"What Emily Card did to bring women access to credit in her work 20 years ago on the Equal Credit Opportunity Act she does now in opening the doors to capital with *Business Capital for Women*. I wish we'd had this book when we started *Ms.* magazine."

—Gloria Steinem

"WOW! The *Our Bodies, Our Selves* for the businesswoman. The authors cover all the relevant, timely topics of capital formation and management needed by the woman business owner of the 90s. Case studies, statistics, resource lists, and tips add icing to the cake. A must-read for the neophyte or struggling business/professional practice owner."

—John May, managing partner, Calvert Social Venture Partners, and co-founder of the Investors' Circle

"Whether they are entrepreneurs, investors, or just women trying to manage their own financial resources or develop them, I know they will find in *Business Capital for Women* a wealth of benefits."

—Adrienne Hall, co-founder, Women Incorporated and co-founder, International Women's Forum

"Emily Card and Adam Miller's insight into the need, sources, and issues concerning women and capital are extraordinary. *Business Capital for Women* presents a major contribution to the understanding, education, and need for action on this topic.

—Edie Fraser, president, Business Women's Network and Public Affairs Group

"A must-have, must-read, must-use reference for all those working to increase the flow of capital to women-led and/or women-owned ventures."

—Liz Harris, vice-president, UNC Partners

"An excellent information source for developing and funding a new business—provides great insight into the entire business development process."

—John O'Toole, senior vice-president, Mellon Equity

BUSINESS CAPITAL
for WOMEN

AN ESSENTIAL
HANDBOOK FOR
ENTREPRENEURS

Emily Card & Adam Miller

MACMILLAN • USA

DISCLAIMER

This publication is designed to provide accurate and authoritative information in regard to the subject matter covered. It is sold with the understanding that neither the author nor the publisher is engaged in rendering legal, accounting, or other professional service. If legal advice or other expert assistance is required, the services of a competent professional person should be sought.

—From a Declaration of Principles Jointly Adopted by a Committee of the American Bar Association and a Committee of Publishers and Associations

MACMILLAN
A Simon & Schuster Macmillan Company
1633 Broadway
New York, NY 10019

Library of Congress Cataloging-in-Publication Data

Card, Emily
    Business capital for woman : an essential handbook for entrepreneurs / Emily Card and Adam Miller.
        p.   cm.
    Includes bibliographical references and index.
    ISBN 0-02-860854-2
    1. Women-owned business enterprises—United States—Finance.
2. Small business—United States—Finance.   I. Miller, Adam (Adam L.)   II. Title.
HG4027.7.C365   1996
658.15′224′024042—dc20   96-22717
                                                                 CIP

Design by Alma Orenstein

10 9 8 7 6 5 4 3 2 1

Printed in the United States of America

ACKNOWLEDGMENTS

Many named and unnamed people provided their insights, expertise, and support for this book. We would like to thank especially:

Denise Marcil, a successful female entrepreneur who is fortunately our agent, and her assistant Jeff Rutherford; John Michel, our editor, for seeing the project to completion; Natalie Chapman for her support of our project when it was just a thought; Claire Caterer for her meticulous line editing of the manuscript and Sharon Lee for producing the book, along with the rest of the Macmillan publication and press departments; Christie W. Kelly, for her endless hours of research, uncovering data in an area where statistics and information, until this publication, were not readily available; Kimberly McGlaughlin, Sarah Cotton, Sharon Fielder, and Roz Kilner for providing assistance in every way as we trudged through the first draft, and Tom Rubin for the same as we worked through the last; and attorneys Jane Katz Crist, Linda Chaplik Harris, Michael Rosenthal; and Marc Andrew Lieberman for serving as expert reviewers; Waldo Card-Brosveen, for once again sharing his thoughts, blankets, remote control, and Captain Crunch, as well as for his understanding of creative space.

Many agencies in Washington provided special help, and we must thank the Small Business Administration and Phil Lader; Amy Millman and Juliette Tracey from the National Women's Business Council; George Stephanoupoulos and Elizabeth Myers at the White House; Mark Schultz of the White House Conference on Small Business; and Lauren Supina of the DNC Women's Leadership Forum.

We are particularly grateful to the members and boards of the Investors' Circle and Capital Circle, many of whom appear in these pages in their roles as business leaders with vision.

A few additional thank you's from Emily: Once again I find myself indebted to formed Senator Bill Brock for his leadership in the area of women's capital access. When I joined Senator Brock's office as a young academic fellow, I never dreaded that over two decades later I would still be involved in the project I began on my first day at work, January 2, 1973. Donna Shalala once said, "Successful academics identify a topic and work it single-mindedly." To the extent that this book makes a contribution, it has been built on that base.

Often the people who have the greatest effect on our perceptions seem, in other ways, so much a part of our lives that we forget to recognize them. Working in my father's drugstore, I saw the daily necessity of meeting payrolls, the practice of staying until the last customer was served, no matter how late, and the never-ending responsibilities of the entrepreneur. Thank you daddy, Ray Watts, for instilling the work ethic. And thanks to David Hill, my father's banker, who opened my first checking account and gave me my first loan. Then there was the Card Family. When Lamar Card and I married, I met a life-long friend who's an entrepreneur to his toes. Whether as a film director and producer or high-tech wizard, Lamar is an "early adopter," and he's had to introduce me to cable, computers, faxes, e-mail, and the Internet. Although we are no longer married, I watch in wonder as Lamar takes each leap forward. His father, Lewis Card Sr., is a down-to-earth genius whose inventions helped create an entire industry, and the late Katherine Card was the first woman I ever saw with an American Express card of her own. Roselia Card has supported my efforts as an ardent reader. My own mother, Anne Dempsey Watts, taught me the most important financial lesson of all, that each individual must have control of her own financial life.

In Los Angeles, many people provided advice and support, including Bob Mayer, negotiator extraordinaire; John Felice, a long-time advisor and friend; and Alex Roldan, Nye Martin, Michael Canale, Irene Malinsky, Rocky Shaheen, George Solorzano, and Cindy Kirven.

Adam would like personally to thank: Ilene and Steven Miller, my parents, for their never-ending love and support, and for not denying or dissuading me from the chance to pursue even the most far-fetched of my endeavors; Perry Wallack, for always sharing anything he had and being ever-willing to lend a helping hand; Larry Witzer, for opening to me his home in the Hills, offering his financial expertise at the poolside, and equipping a writing station on the sundeck; Jon "The Puppet" Tassoff, for his high-tech research assistance and advice; Brian Culot and Andy Millard, my lifelong friends, who could always be counted on for anything, including some much-needed diversions; Adam Fishman, Jenn Rand, Ron Gonen, Lee Wilson, Jay Shiland, Seth Miller, and Rob Cohen, who hosted me from Los Angeles to Washington, D.C., to make our nationwide research effort a reality; all of those who have encouraged me to write, especially Terry Newbold, Celeste Smith, and Sam Culbert; Julianne Sheedy, Julianne Johnson, and Simon & Schuster Australia, for helping with the global editing of the manuscript; Laura Ellington and Adelita Jiménez of Intercultura for their help in Costa Rica; Gus Miller and Henry Weinstein, my grandfathers, for their constant support and encouragement; and the many female entrepreneurs willing to share their thoughts about capital, business, discrimination, hope, and life.

To Marci Miller, Debbie Rubin, Ilene Schlanger, and all the other young women with the independence, ambition, and determination to reach their dreams.

—Adam

To Meta Doherty Carpenter Wilde, a dearly missed friend who reached her dreams and affected all of ours before women dared to dream.

—Emily

CONTENTS

CHAPTER 4 Government Sources of Capital   51

CHAPTER 5 Specialized Sources of Management Development, Capital, and Information   81

INTRODUCTION

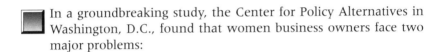

The Capital Gap

In a groundbreaking study, the Center for Policy Alternatives in Washington, D.C., found that women business owners face two major problems:

1. Inadequate access to capital; and
2. The lack of established networks and support systems.

It is not surprising that women face the capital gap. Two decades ago, women could not even get credit cards. With the passage of the Equal Credit Opportunity Act, a new era opened for women's access to the world of finance. That era began with the simple consumer acts of obtaining credit cards and quickly spread to the acquisition of homes by single women. It may be hard to imagine today, but until then so few women bought homes on their own that the census did not even count them until 1980. Now women account for over 35 percent of the condo market.

> **EQUAL CREDIT OPPORTUNITY**
>
> - In 1972, 4.6 percent of American businesses were owned by women.
> - Today the figure stands at over 33 percent.
> - By the year 2000, projected ownership is expected at 40 percent.
>
> *Source: Small Business Administration.*

Horror stories of women being excluded from credit access before the passage of the Equal Credit Opportunity Act in October 1974 hardly seem credible to young women. We cannot imagine a world in which women don't have Visa, Mastercard, and American Express, and yesterday's pariah has become today's target market—at least for consumer credit.

However, women business owners need capital today as much as women consumers needed access to equal credit twenty years ago. You may

> Women's employment has doubled since 1973.
> *Source: Women's Bureau, Department of Labor.*

dream of starting a new business or fantasize about taking you company public, but as a woman, the struggle to gain capital remains your reality. Capital—the money to create, run, and grow your business—has historically been denied to women. Created by outdated economic and social norms, the "capital gap" still remains as a deterrent to female entrepreneurs. This book will show you how to close the capital gap.

> In 1992, receipts for women-owned businesses amounted to $1.6 trillion, yet women are still three times as likely as their male counterparts to start up their businesses using credit cards.
> *Source: National Women's Business Council.*

At a seminar not long ago, we heard a businesswoman ask, "Do we need capital?" Good question. Capital brings complications in the form of control and co-ownership. For many hard-working women entrepreneurs, obtaining capital, along with the associated tradeoffs, may seem to be a step backward. In fact, not all businesses need capital. Some have enough revenues to meet monthly expenses, and the business may run fine without the costs of added capital, which include interest, dividends, and control.

On the other hand, new and growing businesses almost always need more cash. Growing a business without cash limits the size and scope of the operation. And undercapitalized start-up companies do not have the financial strength or flexibility to withstand economic downturns.

Empowering Women with Capital

Today women are changing history. The entry of women into business is the logical conclusion of a

> Women business owners are starting businesses at nearly twice the rate of their male counterparts.
> *Source: Small Business Administration (SBA) Office of Communications and Public Liaison fact sheet, 1995.*

trend that saw the number of women who work and the number of women with children under six years of age in the workplace skyrocket in the same two decades. As women have now seen firsthand the value of the control of capital, starting a business of one's own has become a goal of many teenage girls and corporate executives alike.

Women have realized that one of the fastest ways to the head of the boardroom, one of the easiest ways to improve child care, and one of the most efficient ways to utilize the talents of women is to create and own the companies themselves. But the creation of a company requires more than just vision and drive; it requires money—business capital.

Let's assume you are a midlevel corporate employee with a fantastic idea for a new line of greeting cards. You make $50,000 a year.

Your two children, mortgage, car payment, other family expenses, and taxes run about $40,000 per year. Tired of long hours and inflexible schedules, you want to leave your job to start your own business. You figure at least a year will be needed to generate business income. Yet you need still to support yourself. In addition, to start the business from your home, you need money for a new computer, supplies, and marketing expenses. When considering your income needs and startup costs, your capital requirements are $60,000.

Facing this challenging scenario, many entrepreneurs will blink. If you decide to go ahead, however, your choices include the following:

- Start the business slowly and keep your day job.
- Take out a loan for the materials and supplies.
- Charge the materials and supplies on credit cards.
- Refinance your home, putting the equity into the business.
- Ask your family and friends for loans or investments.
- Ask wealthy individuals you know to invest in the business.
- Go to the bank and obtain a business loan.
- Qualify for a government-backed loan.
- Go to a large greeting card manufacturer and sell the idea to them for part of the ownership.
- Presell the cards and get payment up front. Use that payment to fund the material and supplies.
- Put together a business plan and seek a number of investors.

All of these options can work for anyone starting a business, although credit cards involve high interest and home refinancings place your home at risk. The best choices will partly depend upon the type of business. A high-tech start-up currently has a better chance to use the business plan to seek outside investors. A small boutique might require help from family and friends, at least initially.

> Women business owners employ more people than the Fortune 500 companies employ worldwide, but women-owned businesses receive less than 2 percent of the $2 billion in federal contracts awarded each year.
>
> Source: Small Business Administration, Office of Women's Business Ownership.

Changing Times

Change won't come overnight, but it's happening so fast that perceptions haven't had time to catch up. Those with capital to invest haven't figured out yet what a great opportunity awaits them if they tap into the entrepreneurial zeal of women. Capitalists who invest still look at technological startups as the way to create new fortunes. Informed by history rather than by looking forward to tomorrow, these investors will be caught short unless they turn their attention to the shifting dimensions of entrepreneurship.

Women in business have come to stay, and they are bringing with them new kinds of businesses that offer new products and services to an expanding market long ignored—their own! Just look at Mrs. Fields Cookies. In 1970, who could have predicted that an entire chain of stores would be devoted to cookies? Cookies were bought at bakeries, not at cookie boutiques. Today there are 700 stores in the Mrs. Fields chain. Or look at Betty Nesmith, who used nail polish as her inspiration for creating "liquid paper," eliminating tedious retyping for everyone.

In almost every sector of our small business economy, women's perspectives have reached critical mass. Like all other areas of American life—from law and medicine to the military—where women have entered in great numbers, change is on the way. By the year 2000, when 40 percent of America's small businesses will be in female hands, a transformation will have taken place in our society. Along with these businesses, we'll see new workplace modes and new emphasis on products and services that rise to the challenges facing the marketplace.

Future capital markets will not be able to ignore these small businesses. But for women starting businesses now, the battle is still uphill. Women need every possible advantage in order to overcome the capital gap. Understanding entrepreneurship, the sources of capital, networking, planning, and deal structuring is essential to meeting the challenge. That's what this book is all about.

CHAPTER 1

The World of Capital

The prototypical "women's business" of the 1970s and 1980s—when women netted a third of what men did—won't meet today's female entrepreneurs' dreams. Typically, women- and minority-led businesses bootstrap themselves, using a combination of personal credit cards and mortgage loans to undercapitalize often marginal businesses.

Women today need the tools to launch bigger businesses. When old perceptions of women stood tall as a barrier to capital, it did not make sense for most women to plan ambitious undertakings or to study the world of capital. Today, the growing numbers of female executives, business owners, and business school graduates are causing these outmoded perceptions to crumble. Now you can dream big corporate dreams; and when you do, you can no longer afford to limit your understanding of finance and venture capital.

> Caucasian men represent:
> - 43 percent of the workforce
> - 95 percent of the senior management positions in large companies
>
> Source: "Glass Ceiling Report," Department of Labor, Glass Ceiling Commission, 1995 Report.

To be prepared fully as an entrepreneur, you need to know how to access your financing options. Money awaits—from savings, friends, banks, venture capitalists, the government, and public markets. Regardless of where you eventually get your funding and whether you're looking for start-up money or a strategy to sell your business and cash out your profits, you need to understand the sources of capital.

Capital is the money used to fund every stage of growth of your company.

> By the year 2000, projections suggest that:
> - More than 40 percent of all American businesses will be women-owned.
> - Revenues from these businesses will exceed $1 trillion.
> - The need for women's business capital will continue to rise.
>
> Source: National Women's Business Council.

Generally, capital comes in one of two ways: in the form of debt, which must be repaid (such as a bank loan); or in the form of equity, whose investors share in the profits and ownership of the company (such as venture capital). At each phase of a company's growth there are buyers and sellers, investors looking for investments, and entrepreneurs looking for funding. And at each stage are the players—the bankers, investors, venture capitalists, agents, and entrepreneurs—winding through the world of capital.

The Flow of Capital

Factories. Offices. Equipment. Information. Jobs. Knowledge. These are the products of capital. Interest. Dividends. Options. Gains. These are the returns of capital.

> "Owning capital is not a productive activity."
> —*Joan Robinson*

The flow of capital affects us all. From building financial empires to empowering women to revitalizing communities, it is the flow of capital that defines our tomorrows.

Investors are forever in search of a higher financial return. Although it would appear that eventually all available opportuni-ties would be exhausted, the recent exponential rate of technological advancement has created incredible, unforeseen opportunities daily.

Today returns are not measured merely in terms of their financial value. A growing movement toward socially responsible investing has taken hold. Investments are being judged not only by their potential profits but also by the potential effect on society of flowing capital in that direction.Incorporated within this movement is the desire to provide female and minority entrepreneurs with capital for their businesses.

> "As capitalists increase in any country, the profits which can be made by employing them necessarily diminish. It becomes gradually more and more difficult to find within the country a profitable method of employing any new capital."
> —*Adam Smith, 1776*

Regardless of the type of venture, studies have shown that the empowerment with capital of women and minorities has had a tremendous trickle-down impact on local communities. For example, microloan programs granted by institutions as diverse as a Bangladeshi women's cooperative and the South-shore Bank of Chicago provide business loans as small as fifty or five hundred dollars. To locals struggling to work, these loans have been extremely effective aids in improving their regions' depressed economies.

Barriers to Closing the Capital Gap

Historically, men have controlled capital and directed its flow from investor to company and from company to company. Women have been excluded from the process both because of internal obstacles— women's life-style choices, lack of information, and lack of confidence operating in the male-dominated business world—and external barriers, in particular social, political, and economic norms that said money wasn't ladylike.

Clearly a gap exists between women and men with regard to their access to capital—the ability of the entrepreneur to get money for her business. Why does this gap exist?

Differing World Views

It is hard to say whether the capital gap was started by the societal and psychological differences in men and women or if the gap is just maintained by them. In some cases, historically dictated differences in the positions of men and women still find their expression in modern society. In others, women and men tend to exhibit different approaches to the world around them. These differences, whether derived from culture or socialization, affect women's positions in the business world today. Here are some of the most significant in terms of entrepreneurship:

> **YIN/YANG**
>
> - A businessman is aggressive; a businesswoman is pushy.
> - He isn't afraid to say what he thinks; she's mouthy.
> - He's a stern taskmaster; she's hard to work for.
>
> Source: Marilyn Loden, "How to Tell a Businessman from a Businesswoman," from Feminine Leadership *(New York: Random House, 1985).*

Whether in discussions or in their thinking, men tend to be linear and women tend to be nonlinear. The best expression of this difference is the studies that show the way that men and women find their way in a sensory-deprived darkroom. Men can find their way in the dark through a built-in vectoring system. Women are lost without visual markers (the grocery store on the corner, the flower shop in the middle of the block, the dogwood tree in the yard).

Males have a tendency to posture when an answer isn't known. Women posture less frequently, instead admitting they don't know. Just get lost when driving somewhere and see who asks for directions first. This style difference confuses both women and men. Men assume women know far less than they do. Women assume men know more than they do.

> "If a man mulls over a decision, they say, 'He's weighing the options.' If a woman does it they say, 'She can't make up her mind.'"
>
> —Barbra Streisand

> A study of college students attempted to show that highly educated young women are no longer submissive in discussions with male peers, but the results did not support the original hypothesis. Researchers found, "the men tended to set the agenda by offering opinions, suggestions, and information. The women tended to react, offering agreement or disagreement."
>
> Source: Deborah Tannen, You Just Don't Understand (New York: Ballantine Books, 1990), p. 129.

Men and women have different business styles. Meetings often clearly reveal gender differences in approach. Men think in terms of a linear agenda with an up or down vote; women think in terms of producing consensus on each point before moving ahead. Men's perceptions of women in meetings is that they babble (consensus building). Women's perceptions of men in meetings is that they posture, restating the obvious (majority building).

Popular images of an "entrepreneur" can also affect capital access: At a venture fair for high-tech companies, a CEO presenting breakthrough technologies arrived dressed in a proper business suit but with hair streaming to her waist. In the evaluation session, the men in the audience commented more on her hair than on her company. Some would argue that such anachronistic male behavior doesn't deserve respect, while others suggest that for the moment, women need to attend to the dominant venture modes.

Internal Barriers

The single largest constraint to capital for women is a general lack of awareness of the sources of capital. Due to a lack of experience, mentors, research, and available information, as well as acculturation discouraging involvement in business and finance, many women do not know how to apply for a commercial loan or how to utilize the Small Business Administration; nor do they understand what an investment banker does. Understanding the available sources of capital is essential to accessing them. If you don't know it's there, you certainly won't be able to find it. The following chapters are meant to help overcome this problem. A separate chapter is devoted to each general source of capital: personal, private, government, not-for-profit, business, and public.

> "Half of all businesses are minority- or women-owned. It's where jobs are created and the economy is based. It's a market that must be targeted by financial institutions. Government needs to look at the service end of the economy (not just sexy high-tech). And women have to take themselves seriously, aim high, take risks, find their niche in the economy, and seek resources to strengthen their capacity."
>
> —Hedy Ratner, director, Women's Business Development Center, Chicago

Many women are not fully prepared when soliciting potential investors. Whether or not women in general have had experience, mentors, or information, *you* need to be prepared when confronting investors and bankers. Even if you want to start a small lifestyle business to suit your personal and family needs, you should understand the stages of financing your venture and the potential sources of that financing.

Many women business owners exhibit less self-confidence than their male counterparts.   Some women argue that they have been acculturated to be less self-confident. Others say women are less self-confident because they do not adequately prepare themselves to start their businesses and raise capital, do not have mentors, or both.

The lack of self-confidence mani-fests itself in direct and measurable

> "Women are still afraid of money. I am."
> —*Hazel A. King, successful small-business owner*

ways. Female entrepreneurs tend to start small sole proprietorships and partnerships rather than midsize or larger corporations. These small, usually service-oriented businesses have few assets, which means little collateral. And because small start-ups don't require much money, most banks aren't willing to expend the administrative time necessary to approve the loan.

By fully planning the venture, meeting the right people, and responding to the demands of the world of capital, you will not only prepare yourself to raise capital but you will better position your venture for success.

External Barriers

The lack of awareness of services and capital available to women business owners is not limited to inexperienced entrepreneurs or par-ticular programs and organizations. *The convoluted, overwhelming, and undermarketed web of programs for women is difficult to comprehend.* To further confuse the situation, a distinct lack of consolidated informa-tion has prevented women from easily understanding the female business arena, particularly as it relates to capital access.

Many potential investors, particularly institutional lenders, do not take women seriously.   Some men, particularly older men, still have a bias against women in business. Others just don't feel that women are credible, and even some female bankers agree. Initiating the loan process without a business plan or get-ting personally offended by standard loan application questions further hurts your ability to negotiate. In the short term, women can best combat these misperceptions by being prepared physically, mentally, and emotionally, and having the confidence to demand equal treatment for themselves.

> Faye Allison Heller was turned down for a bank loan each time she went to finance a new truck for her company. Even though she had contracts, had a successful track record, and would earn more than her husband, the bank again demanded that her husband cosign the loan for her fourth truck. Frustrated, she warned, "If you make me cosign, I'll go somewhere else." They didn't.
>
> Source: *Interview with Faye Allison Heller, CEO, Philly Fasteners, Inc.*

Women do not have sufficient female mentors and role models to show them how to move ahead. Today this problem can be overcome with business development information specifically targeted for women. More and more women's networking organizations include successful female entrepreneurs, and progress is being made on the government front to specifically promote women in business. In addition, committed young women have found men as willing as women to serve as mentors.

Stages of a Business

Like all of us, a company goes through stages in its life: conception, birth, growth, maturity, and death. And like people, not every company hits each stage at the same time, in the same way, or at all.

Start-up

The start-up of a company actually involves a series of distinct phases, each of which brings your venture from conception to reality.

CONCEPTION

We all have ideas. Every day we go to stores that we could better manage, we go to restaurants that we could better design, we see movies that we could better produce, and we envision products that everyone would want. Or at least that's what we think.

> "There is always plenty of capital for those who can create practical plans for using it."
> —Napoleon Hill

The conception of a venture goes much further than these passing thoughts. The concept becomes a recurring fantasy, each time becoming more defined. You start thinking about the consequences of your vision, the impact its implementation could have on your life, and potential sources of capital. You start talking about your ideas to your friends. Eventually, you put your thoughts on paper and create a complete business plan.

During the business planning process, the viability of your concept should become clear. You will begin forming a management team and working with your potential partners. You will work through the specifics of your plan—choosing sites, determining capital requirements, and developing marketing and operational plans.

IMPLEMENTATION

Often, the single biggest step for the individual is from conception to implementation. It is implementation that separates the dreamer from the entrepreneur.

Reaching implementation involves details. By the time you implement your plan, chances are you have refined your business plan several times. Assumptions have changed, plans had to be compromised with reality, delays have thrown off your timeline, and cash constraints have limited your purchasing power.

> "'Everything's going fine,' she said. 'There are only a few details to finish up.'
>
> "At this the teacher scratched his head. 'Only a few details?' he asked, looking puzzled. 'But details are all there are.'"
>
> —from Rick Fields, Chop Wood, Carry Water (Los Angeles: Jeremy P. Tarcher, 1984), p. 124.

Depending on your venture, your implementation stage can be long or short and may involve varying levels of capital, research, construction, and equipment.

High-tech companies usually need a fair amount of equipment to initiate operations, but often have the advantage of limited space and personnel requirements. According to the Small Business Administration, 70 percent of all high-tech firms have fewer than twenty employees.

Retail operations often live and die by the location chosen. Although construction may be warranted in certain cases, buying an existing retail space or restaurant and modifying it for your specific purpose tends to be the most effective approach. Of course, if you are taking another's retail space, particularly if it housed the same type of operation, you should seriously consider why the space became available. Did problems stem from management or the location and market? As you move toward opening day, you will need to begin staffing the stores and filling the shelves, so your focus eventually will shift from the abstract to personnel, inventory, and cash-flow management.

Service businesses enjoy virtually immediate operation. Consulting and legal work can be done from your house, in your client's office, or in local restaurants at lunch meetings. Other professionals prefer to join their peers in professional office buildings with shared libraries, receptionists, and facilities. Aside from schooling, the biggest expense (until expansion forces high overhead) tends to be client recruitment. The up side is, with your first client, you're in business.

RAMPING-UP

The adrenaline rush from your first order is exactly what you need to carry you through the next fast-paced stage of your start-up. Once you have the green light to operate, whether you had been waiting for regulatory approval from the government, capital from your investors, or simply the first large order of your product, it is time to "ramp-up."

Ramping-up involves getting the equipment and the personnel necessary to operate. Although manufacturing ventures typically

require the most preparation to begin operations, all start-up companies have some amount of ramping-up before they get off the
ground. Service companies may need to advertise and train before
taking on clients. Restaurant and retail store managers need to remodel
or construct the location, hire staff, and fill the shelves. Media companies may take months in production and post-production after developing content. Biotech ventures may be in years of development
before suddenly having to ramp-up immediately to manufacture newly
created drugs.

Of course, preparation is not limited to start-up companies. Even
mature manufacturing companies may have to ramp-up with the
introduction of new products or the acceptance of custom orders.

Growth

The growth stage can be at once the most exciting and, like puberty,
the most difficult. During the growth of your venture, you will be
expanding your operations, increas-
ing staff, enlarging your office or
opening multiple locations, and wid-
ening your customer base.

> "If you divorce capital from labor, capital is hoarded, and labor starves."
> —Daniel Webster

Never-ending growth of your com-
pany is not always desirable. In the first place, cash is often burned at
a rapid rate to fuel the growth. For this reason, the rising value of the
company on the balance sheet is not necessarily reflected in the bank
statements. The cash crunch can be observed in many publicly held
growth companies that offer high returns but no dividends because
the cash is used internally to finance growth. In addition, the increased pressures of rapid expansion can lead to endless management
and operational strains. Given this cash-flow problem and the
management difficulties, high-growth ventures do not make for good
life-style businesses.

One other problem threatens entrepreneurial founders of high-
growth companies. The success of your venture may start your
shareholders calling for "professional management." Shareholders,
directors, and investors may fear that the same technological or artis-
tic leanings that made you a great force breathing sustainable life into
your venture hamper the handling and the management of a full-
scale corporation.

> Sandra Kurtzig, the president of ASK Computer Systems, turned $2,000 into $66.9 million in just 10 years.
> Source: Earl C. Gottschalk, Jr., Wall Street Journal, 17 May 1983, p. 1.

Of course, there are benefits to
growth. By the growth stage, your
dream has become a successful reality. You may now be earning more
than your coworkers at your old job.
Your investors are pleased with their
returns (although they inevitably

want more). Your employees respect your ability to create a large-scale operation from scratch. And you should, by now, have faith in your own instincts.

Maturity

Few companies reach the maturity stage. Most have died soon after implementation or have burned out in a flash of growth. Many of those that survive become the corporate giants that dominate the economy.

Matured companies tend to be large, low-growth, high-volume operations. Profit gains are often limited to cost reductions rather than increased sales. Usually having gone public during the growth stage, matured companies typically are capitalized through a combination of institutional financing and public debt and equity. Large bureaucracies, which have developed over time, are typically regrettably slow to respond to employees, markets, and change. In most cases, the entrepreneurial founders of the company have exited, replaced by large, professional management teams and amorphous corporate boards.

Because internal growth is often limited by the size of the market, many mature companies target corporate acquisitions for diversity and earnings. In some cases, the entrepreneur or her successors to the matured company make acquisitions that comply more with their personal interests than with their company's operations. For example, Edgar Bronfman Jr., the heir to Seagram's, a liquor company, was driven by his fascination with Hollywood to purchase entertainment giant MCA.

Exit Strategy

An essential component of entrepreneurial vision is the exit strategy to convert the value of the company to cash for the entrepreneur and her investors. Shareholders want to know that their investment and effort will convert to tangible returns.

To support growth, many successful ventures choose to continually reinvest their profits rather than distribute the profits to the owners. As a result, entrepreneurs usually do not personally receive the full monetary benefits of their company's success until they "exit" or leave the company.

Several different strategies are available to the entrepreneur for cashing out. The favored exit strategy for most venture capitalists is the initial public offering or IPO. Through an

> In 1992, almost 600 companies raised a total of $39.4 billion through initial public offerings.
>
> Source: Bill Graham, "The Year in IPO's," Inc., May 1993, vol. 13, no. 5, p. 157.

initial public offering, the company goes public and has its shares traded on a stock exchange. The original shareholders can either sell off their shares or trade them in for stock of the now public company. To determine the price per share of the company at the time of the offering, the company is valued primarily based on expectations of future growth and success. As a result, shareholders of high-growth companies get a handsome return for their interest in the venture— often receiving publicly traded stock twenty or thirty times the value of their original investment.

Other companies seek to be acquired. By selling the company at a multiple of revenues (two to three times) or earnings (five to seven times), the true value of the venture can be captured. In many cases, the seller actually wants to stay on board with the company, at least for another few years. Because the high costs of an IPO are avoided, this option is quite attractive to successful entrepreneurs who get to cash out and keep their jobs.

Still other entrepreneurs prefer instead to reap the benefits over time. Management looks to the company as a "cash cow" that can be milked at any time. Instead of using the revenues to grow the company, the owners prefer to stabilize the company and grow their bank accounts.

Stages of Capital

Although there are exceptions, the stages of capital roughly follow the stages of business. *Seed* capital is sought by entrepreneurs with a concept; *start-up* capital is sought by new ventures ramping-up for operation; *mezzanine* or *expansion* capital is sought by growing and mature companies. *Bridge* financing, which may be sought at any level, are funds meant to bridge the gap between today and tomorrow's expected financing.

Seed Capital

You have the perfect concept and you're ready to move. The problem is, if you leave your job now, you won't have any income until the venture is funded and operational. If you try to start the company while you are working, both your work and your family will suffer. How do entrepreneurs solve this initial financing problem? Seed capital.

The reality is, the most probable source of seed capital is personal. Most investors and venture capitalists will *not* give you money to let you develop your idea. In fact, most potential investors will want to see a sacrifice on your part. They want to see you put up, or obtain through personal resources, seed capital. They also want to see your sacrifice in terms of sweat equity. In other words, most potential investors will expect to see you devote your full attention to the venture (so no other jobs) and provide seed capital (without income from another job).

Sound impossible? Welcome to the world of venture capital. There are many potential solutions to the problem, including the following:

- You can save enough money while you are working to carry you through the initial stages of the venture.
- You could get seed capital from your family, usually your parents. (Note: This is one reason why disadvantaged children face additional difficulties becoming successful entrepreneurs. They do not have the time or resources necessary to explore their entrepreneurial ideas.)
- You may have a venture that can start up quickly or inexpensively, eliminating the need for any substantial amount of seed capital.

What if you are facing a long development timeline because of the size of your financing needs or operational requirements, and you have no source of seed money? Well, you have two options, neither of which are very appealing. You can abandon your plans or go into high-interest credit card debt. Either option is risky. Unfortunately, the inability to obtain seed financing or the time to develop a new venture idea is the single biggest barrier to entrepreneurship and small-business creation.

Start-up Capital

In order to get your venture fully operational, you need financing. You will need money for equipment, offices, staff, marketing, and supplies. In other words, you need capital to start up. Although similar, seed capital and start-up capital should be distinguished. Seed capital, used to fully develop a concept, can normally be funded only through personal sources. By contrast, start-up capital used to get your venture off the ground can usually be obtained through a variety of private and government sources.

Start-up capital is the backbone of venture capital; it is the money invested in an idea in the hope of high returns. Interestingly, and unfortunately, most venture capital firms have moved away from investing start-up capital, which has proven too risky for many firms. Instead they have turned to investing in the later stages of fully operational ventures. Because banks have also historically shunned venture capital investments, private investors and government funds have become the most available sources of start-up venture capital today.

Depending on your venture, your start-up capital requirements can vary tremendously. A service firm may only need a minimum

> Fred Smith received $90 million in start-up capital to create Federal Express.
>
> Source: Federal Express.

amount of capital to initiate operations with a complete office and staff until revenues are high enough to internally finance operations and growth. A high-tech firm may need a few hundred thousand dollars to fund the research and development required to bring a new product to market. An international manufacturing venture may require several million dollars to become fully operational. Of course, to get financing, the size of your expected returns must match the amount of your funding requests.

Investors expect the distribution of start-up capital to be staged. Even if you will ultimately receive $2 million in start-up capital, it probably will come in stages with operational benchmarks at each stage. For example, the first $250,000 may be available to develop special pagers for moms and their kids. Once developed, another $500,000 will be available to acquire equipment, a manufacturing plant, and office space. Then $750,000 will be released to complete your ramp-up, buy supplies, hire workers, and produce 500,000 pagers. Finally, another $500,000 will be available to market and distribute the pagers as well as to secure a working capital line of credit.

STARTING CAPITAL REQUIREMENTS OF WOMEN-OWNED BUSINESSES: 1982–1987

Among those women who did require start-up capital, over two-thirds (67.6 percent) did not use borrowed capital, 9.4 percent borrowed less than half of the capital required to start their businesses, 13 percent borrowed more than half, and 10 percent borrowed all of the capital required to start the business.

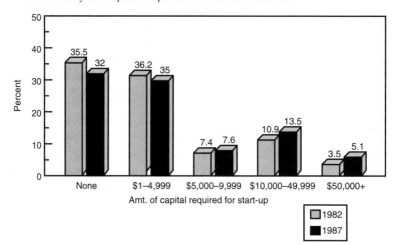

Source: Bureau of the Census

Mezzanine Financing

Should your venture prove successful, you will inevitably need more money to grow. Although much of your growth can be internally financed through the company's operational revenues, significant growth normally requires outside financing. You may decide to open other locations nationwide, distribute your product internationally, or acquire suppliers and competitors to increase sales and improve efficiency.

Mezzanine financing provides companies the fuel to grow. Because the venture is on its second, third, or fourth round of financing, a wide array of financing options *should* be available. In some cases, entrepreneurs don't plan properly for future financial requirements and thus cut off potential sources of funding. It's important always to strive to preserve the future financial flexibility of the company. For example, if the company is overleveraged at the outset, banks and bonds will be effectively excluded from the mezzanine rounds. If too much equity was given up by you at the formation of the company, there won't be a sufficient percentage of the company left to entice equity or venture capital investors at the mezzanine round.

Today, most venture capital firms focus on mezzanine financing. By investing in later-round financing, the firms have a company track record on which to base their investment decisions. Some firms focus on particular industries while others may focus on specific types of mezzanine financing, such as acquisition financing used by one company to buy another.

Bridge Financing

The process of raising money takes time. Even when you have solid financing leads, it could take months for the cash to reach your hands. In the interim you may need capital to carry you over the waiting period. You may need what is called *bridge financing*.

Bridge financing is often readily available. Even the investor with whom you are negotiating may offer to help you until the lingering deal is closed. But beware: Bridge loans are rarely cheap, and it is often better to cut costs and struggle through the waiting period than to risk the additional terms and interest expense of a bridge loan.

Sources of Capital

The money for your business can come from many different places. Most ventures are funded by a combination of sources, including any or all of the following:

- *Personal* savings and sweat equity, or your unpaid hours, are an expected component of your financing. Even if your company is eventually fully funded, you will inevitably have dedicated time and effort toward developing the concept. Commercial loans and investments by friends and family are potentially available but involve a significant amount of personal risk. Of course, if you join an existing venture, you may be able to avoid direct personal investment, but some level of personal sacrifice is normally involved.
- *Private* venture capital is available in many forms. Venture capital (VC) firms are the traditional source of funding for new ventures, but they have become increasingly hesitant to fund the initial stages of growth and typically are extremely demanding in their terms. In addition to VC firms, wealthy individual investors, whose behaviors range from passive to obstructive, fund ventures for profit and sport.

VENTURE CAPITAL POOL

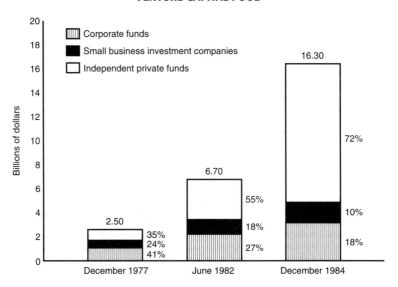

Source: Capital Publishing Corp., Venture Capital Journal; see also 1986 Report to the President, The State of Small Business, p. 58.

- *Government* funding usually comes disguised. The government may be your first buyer or otherwise make a procurement deal with your company. The Small Business Administration might guarantee a commercial loan made by your bank. Or your venture capitalist may have gotten two times the money in her venture fund from the Small Business Administration through a Small Business Investment Company.

- *Nonprofit* organizations and foundations have programs designed to assist entrepreneurs. Many of these programs specifically focus on helping women with managing and funding their ventures.
- *Business* financing arrives when companies are willing to put up part or all of the company to get some money. Companies may decide to partner together in return for financing, profit, or strategic advantage. Other businesses choose to factor or sell their accounts receivable to get financing. Still other companies bootstrap, barter, franchise, and otherwise creatively finance their ventures.
- *Public* money, the heart of Wall Street, is normally reserved for successful, high-growth companies. Whether you issue stocks or bonds, you can be sure that lawyers, bankers, accountants, the Securities and Exchange Commission (SEC), and big money are involved.

STAGING YOUR SOURCES OF CAPITAL

Stage of Business	Type of Capital	Typical Source of Investment	Chapter
Conception	Seed	Personal	2
Implementation	Start-up	Savings	2
		Banks	2
		Government (loan guarantees)	4
		Friends and family	2
		Credit cards	2
		Individual investors	3
		Foundations and corporations	5
Ramping-up	Start-up	Same	2, 3, 4, 5
Growth	Mezzanine	Banks	2
		Venture capital firms	3
		Receivables/inventory financing firms	6
Maturity	Mezzanine	Venture capital firms	3
		Commercial loans	2
		Internal (business financing)	6

Investors

An obviously key element of the world of capital are the lenders and investors themselves. Understanding the type of investor you deal with will often help you in your negotiations.

Types of Investors

Unless you limit your capital needs to your savings account, you will have to work with others to finance your venture. Every potential source of capital has gatekeepers who control the investment decision-making. The roles of these gatekeepers vary.

Venture capitalists place money in high-risk ventures or new businesses. They live and work in the world of capital. They see hundreds of business plans and entrepreneurs. Because of their experience and sophistication, venture capitalists search for potential high-growth ventures that they can take public within five to seven years. Often thought ruthless, venture capitalists typically demand extremely high returns and control of your company. Depending on the firm's policies and the venture capitalists' style, they may also demand participation in your venture's management. In other cases, they take a more passive position unless and until the venture fails to produce expected returns. Venture capital firms tend to specialize either in a particular region, where they can maximize the benefit of their contacts or, in a particular industry, where they can take advantage of the firm's expertise.

Solo venture capitalists invest their own money in high-risk ventures. Because they are investing only their own money, they have no fiduciary obligations and are extremely involved personally in their investments. They also tend to have high personal net worths. Self-made solo venture capitalists usually prefer to invest in the industries where they made their own fortunes and usually become involved in the operational plans of the venture.

Private investors are less experienced, but normally more excited, about venture capital investing. Typically, private investors have limited investment experience in venture capital but have a strong interest in a particular company or industry. Because they have less experience than venture capitalists, they tend to be less sophisticated in their review of companies. The source of their investment funds may be self-made or through inheritance.

Be careful when choosing private investors. Some unsophisticated private investors searching for a pet company of their own become a nuisance to the operation of the company; these investors often wield the power of the purse without any real understanding of the operation and without any management experience.

Family fund managers take control of investing their family's wealth. Depending on their personal level of experience, these managers can come off as sophisticated investors or spoiled, rich kids. Family funds are often a kind of hybrid, part venture capital fund and part private investor—they are a venture fund of one family's investment capital. Just as venture capital firms do, family funds tend to be regional or focused on particular industries.

Institutional lenders or bankers are, by nature, usually the most conservative group you will meet. The purpose of their job is to minimize risk when issuing loans, so don't expect them to

> Patriarchy assumes that women will either marry or fall under the protection of a male. The male protector may take the shape of relative, priest, trustee, or banker.

be as excited as you about your financial projections. Commercial bankers will usually base their lending decisions on your personal credit history and available collateral—not on the expected viability of your venture. Unless you are highly capitalized from the outset, these bankers will not seriously consider lending to your company, as opposed to you, until your venture reaches the growth stage.

Government agents or bureaucrats, once you reach them, are usually quite helpful. The problem when dealing with large, bureaucratic agencies is to get in contact with the right person. Often the red tape and phone transfers can wear you down before you obtain any substantial help. By understanding the types of programs available and the places to find them, you will have a distinct advantage in the governmental arena.

Corporate agents, who represent corporate investment funds, vary as much as the companies with which you deal. Some nonprofit and for-profit development companies are geared to deal specifically with women and will be quite cognizant of your needs and concerns. Other corporate agents are more interested in placing their cash in safe, short-term investments and won't be responsive to your solicitations for capital.

Investment bankers are a special breed. As the people who place public and private capital in investments, they are the gatekeepers of Wall Street. Unlike commercial bankers, investment bankers work much like lawyers or consultants would. Investment bankers specialize in areas such as

> "Women need to learn what Wall Street does even if you are getting the money from your friends. Underwriters raise the money. If you are planning for success, you will need to hit the Street sooner or later."
>
> —*Michael Faber, private investor, in* Interview, *May 1995*

corporate finance, emerging markets, public finance, and high-yield debt, and they use their financial expertise to advise their corporate, government, and entrepreneurial clients. Corporate-side investment bankers daily structure multimillion-dollar private and public offerings, match successful ventures with investors, and advise companies on mergers and acquisitions. In general, the high cost of investment bankers makes their services prohibitive to small start-up ventures, but they are essential when funding a large venture or when making a high-growth company public.

Women Investing in Women

Despite the fact that women hold almost half of the privately held capital in the United States, primarily due to inheritance, only recently have women significantly become serious investors. Primarily, the cause can be attributed to the fact that women owned but did not control the wealth that was left to them by their husbands or fathers. In this generation, for the first time we have seen widows inheriting capital outright and female executives and entrepreneurs making enough money to become investors.

Although few female investors concentrate exclusively on women, many sophisticated investors are beginning to make investing in women a priority. As women continue to take a firmer hold in the business world, so too will women become stronger in the investment community. Inroads Capital, with a $50 million venture fund, has taken the lead as one of the first venture capital firms to specifically target women-owned companies. Eventually, women (and men) investing in women will abound, but that transition will take time.

WOMEN'S AND MEN'S SHARES OF SOLE PROPRIETORSHIPS, 1977–2005

According to the National Association of Women Business Owners, women-owned businesses employ 35 percent more workers than all Fortune 500 companies worldwide.

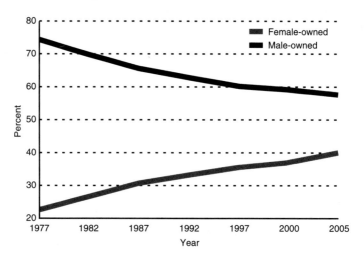

Source: Small Business Administration (SBA), Office of Advocacy.

To speed up the process, one challenge women face is to use their entrepreneurial creativity to develop new investment vehicles for small businesses. The reality is, with almost 40 percent of all businesses and an even larger percentage of start-ups now being women-owned, increasing the amount of capital available to small businesses inevitably increases the capital flowing to women-owned businesses. Recognizing this effect, an important focus for women at the 1995

White House Conference on Small Business was on capital formation in general, not specifically for women.

One push is to direct more pension-fund investments to small businesses. Another is venture collateral being de-

> Of $892.6 billion in public pension fund investments, only $5.46 billion was invested in small businesses. That is only 0.6 percent of all public pension fund investments.
>
> *Source: Small Business Administration, Office of Advocacy*

veloped in Philadelphia by Women's Collateral Funding, Inc. Encouragement of bank microloan programs also would improve the available capital for some female entrepreneurs. Finally, completely new investment instruments, such as stacked bank loans, where multiple ventures submit a combined application, or women-directed community venture pools need to be explored and developed.

Resources and References

Eric Flamholtz's *Growing Pains* (San Francisco: Jossey-Bass, 1990) explains the typical growing pains facing managers of growth-stage companies. Regardless of the type of venture you manage, the growing pains you will face transcend industry boundaries.

For a more complete comparison of management styles of men and women, see The National Foundation of Women Business Owners' *Styles of Success* (Washington, D.C.: The National Foundation of Women Business Owners, 1994).

Resources for each general source of capital will be given at the end of the following chapters. To learn more about the different types of investors, network with them. Developing relationships with investors in different areas is essential to funding your venture. After all of the due diligence is done, people invest in people, often people they know. If you're concerned about your lack of knowledge, visit banks, brokers, and venture capitalists when you are out of town to get the "stupid" questions out of the way. If you are sincere, these people will usually be more than willing to talk.

CHAPTER 2

Personal Sources of Capital

Statistics show the primary source of capital for most female entrepreneurs has been personal. Whether in the form of sweat equity, savings, credit cards, loans from family and friends, or loans and credit lines from the local bank, women barred from accessing traditional sources of venture capital have turned to their own resources.

In reality, men too have been required to put up their share of personal resources into any new venture. The difference is, for most men, personal capital has been a beginning, the seed money for the venture; for most women, personal capital has been both the beginning and the end.

Sweat Equity

Properly the starting point for any business is "sweat equity," or the ideas, commitment, energy, and human capital of the entrepreneur herself. If you think starting a business means

> "I will not quit, I will not quit, I will not quit until I die."
>
> —*Entrepreneur Judy Ets-Hokin at the Capital Circle*

setting your own schedule, you're right. You'll have the freedom to set your schedule—for longer hours, harder work, and dealing with details you never dreamed of. You'll learn the ins and outs of your (usually outdated) equipment. Kinko's or its equivalent will, indeed, become your "branch office."

Sweat equity is the free time you devote to your venture. "Free" time because you either are not getting paid or are severely underpaid for the work you do on behalf of the venture. The theory is that a devoted entrepreneur is willing to accept the tasks because she has equity in the company and will benefit from the company's success as the owner. In essence, the value of the entrepreneur's services, the amount she would be paid for the work she did, is part of the entrepreneur's personal capital contribution to the company.

Although it doesn't appear on any charts showing the sources of start-up capital, sweat equity is part of every venture. Sweat equity is vital in recruiting other forms of capital. By showing your commitment to the venture, you show that the venture has become part of you. People do not want to invest in your hobby; they want to invest in you.

Psychic Equity

In addition to the sweat and blood you dedicate to your venture, there are psychic costs to starting a company. The hours your children are at school become the most precious part of the business day. Many times you'll have to turn down a breakfast meeting because you have another breakfast meeting at home with your six- and ten-year-olds. Or a request for a drink after work gives way to a homework session for the paper on colonial America that your sixth grader must deliver the next day. In the fall, Halloween costumes are sandwiched between business meetings. Holiday shopping becomes catalog shopping. Soon guilt is added to your list of worries. You slog on, sure that success, or at least the first positive sign, is just around the next corner.

Long hours and hard work are the cornerstones of any business start-up effort. Capital is not a substitute for the commitment of the entrepreneur herself. When you add employees, this commitment becomes even more critical. When employees leave for the day, the entrepreneur's work is usually about half done. Literally and figuratively, only you will open the doors and lock them at night. By your example, you'll inspire the others around you to work long hours with short pay.

> Karen Stevenson, a business school professor at UCLA, teaches that you need to use your "personal power," not your "positional power" or title, to get the performance you need in a start-up business setting.

Don't expect the fact that you are president of the company to automatically confer employee respect. You need to inspire your workers through your actions and earn their respect rather than forcing your position on them. Although this concept is important to any manager or leader, it is critical when working in a small-business environment. Working side by side with your sleeves rolled up doesn't mesh with throwing your weight around.

Savings

More than time and commitment will be needed for your business. At the minimum, you'll have telephone, paper, photocopying, and postage expenses. Most small businesses gain great competitive advantage by owning at least one good computer with all the trimmings, so there are also minimum equipment expenses. You also may need to purchase raw materials for a factory, lease retail space for a boutique, or have other start-up costs.

> "If you don't have capital and haven't planned for your own business, get another job. Wait until you have the capital and the equipment first."
>
> —Lois Carter Fay, entrepreneur

All of these initial expenses need to be financed somehow. Savings provide the safest place to start. If you have been able to save enough from your employment income, starting a business presents much less risk than if you need other investors from the outset. Without other investors, you can retain complete control over your company. And by using your savings instead of loans, you will avoid interest payments that can quickly eat into your cash flow. Of course, you should try to avoid using any retirement funds you've put away, particularly if you are starting later in life. As you age, that money becomes increasingly difficult to replace.

You will have to cover your lost salary until your business produces income. At a minimum, you should have enough capital to cover all your costs—including your own living expenses—for six months. But depending on the business, it can take two or three years before you reach the break-even point, including your own salary.

> "Very carefully estimate the operating capital you will need. Then multiply by three."
>
> —Sylvia Sarafian, computer software businesswoman, quoted in Emily Card, "The Business Plan," Ms. magazine, November 1985

When you can amass enough savings before you start the business, you improve your position, regardless of the venture's outcome. If you succeed, it will be all yours. If not, you will have limited the downside risk to the amount in your bank account.

Friends and Family

Turning to those who know you best and believe in you—your friends and family—represents a time-honored source of capital. Borrowing or obtaining equity from your nearest and dearest may be the easy route to funding—or a quick route to family hell.

If the business goes well, your supporters will be grateful to have been included. If your business does not meet success, you'll hear about it at Thanksgiving dinner for the next twenty years.

Although getting family money may seem like an easy route to start-up funding, tread carefully before taking the dough. Formalize your handshake promises in writing with either stocks or a promissory note. In this way, if the business fails, at least your relatives will have a write-off on their tax return.

Be scrupulous with the people you would normally treat informally. Provide them with updates of your progress in writing. If at all possible, take the money in the form of loans that you will pay back in a timely fashion; otherwise, you can provide your friendly investors with an equity position in, or share of, the company.

With these cautions in mind, money from family and friends certainly has a role to play in start-up financing. As with any other prospective investor, your relatives and friends will want to be assured that you have taken the risk along with them. Don't expect Uncle Johnny to cough up his last twenty thousand if you haven't put in your five.

Seller Financing

If your new business opportunity comes from purchasing someone else's ongoing enterprise, seller financing is the way to go. If the business has the basics in place, then once you and the seller agree on a valuation, you buy the business through an agreed-on installment plan. In other words, you pay a down payment to take control of the business and sign an interest-bearing note to the seller for the remaining cost of the business.

Buying an existing business also has other advantages. Whether it is a toy store with a complete inventory or a dental practice, once you identify an opportunity that excites you, the chances for financing—as well as success—will be improved. By taking on an existing concern, you'll have a built-in measure of success. But be wary of why the business is being sold; there may be hidden flaws in the market or the operation, or the business may not be able to support the additional cash needed to cover the seller's loan.

Commercial Loans

In television advertisements for commercial loans, the banker looks like your best friend. You know the ad—the anxious entrepreneur goes in to meet a smiling banker who both understands her business and approves the loan. The reality, unfortunately, is often quite different. Despite an increase in the number of women-owned firms, women's access to commercial loans declined by 8 percent in the five years from 1982 to 1987.

Commercial loans are covered under the Equal Credit Opportunity Act (ECOA), but certain antidiscrimination provisions are not as stringent for business loans, leading to the possibility of lender discrimination against women. In addition, smaller commercial loans are actually handled in the consumer lending division of most banks. In a consumer lending division, ECOA protection is stronger, but credit criteria are tougher, too. In some banks, the potential businessperson seeking a loan of $100,000 or less is grouped with consumers rather than being batched with other entrepreneurs who similarly have strong credentials but some blemishes on their records. Ironically, in these divisions the antidiscrimination laws are given as the reason for denying loans to entrepreneurs without perfect records. The rationale: If a lender doesn't make comparable consumer loans to other bank customers with similar track records, they can't grant them to you.

> "Because women business owners tend to be concentrated in small businesses with relatively low funding needs and in industries lacking traditional collateral, they tend to be unattractive to lenders."
>
> —*National Women's Business Council*, Report to the President *(Washington, D.C.: NWBC, 1992), 6*

Similar to a commercial loan is a *line of credit*. The bank uses essentially the same valuation methods to approve the line of credit, but the venture takes the money, up to the credit limit, only as needed. Like a credit card, interest is charged only on the money actually used. Some revolving credit lines, which work much like American Express but with interest, require repayment of money borrowed every sixty or ninety days.

Letters of credit will be required if your business involves international transactions. A letter of credit is a line of credit which you actually never use—it operates as a guarantee by the bank to your international sellers as your transaction moves through the international banking sphere. For doing business abroad, get to know the federal Import-Export Bank. This agency serves small and large businesses alike and helps to ensure that exporters and importers obtain letters of credit with favorable terms.

Criteria for Commercial Loans

Commercial lenders generally make their decisions on a variety of factors, including your income, credit record, business plan, business sector, entrepreneurial track record, experience within the business sector, and asset-to-debt ratio (usually a minimum of three to one).

Lenders require an enormous amount of documentation for loans because the banking regulatory agencies require it. Without properly requiring such documentation, the country risks finding itself in the

BANK LOANS AND A SUPPORTIVE SPOUSE

Diane Lipton Dennis, Lipton Corporate Child Care Centers, Inc. Washington

When an employee's regular child-care arrangements fall through, corporations face major costs and time losses as a result of absenteeism. Backup child care is therefore a major problem for American business. But it's also one of those hidden market opportunities that women, with their unique perspective, are in a position to see and exploit. Rather than become another victim to child-care emergencies, one woman put her energies into solving the problem.

Diane Lipton Dennis realized in 1990 that she wanted to start a company that would become the premiere provider of turnkey corporate backup child care. Formerly an executive with a major national child-care chain, Dennis had both the expertise necessary to put together a service that would meet the needs of parents in executive positions and the business acumen to make the centers instantly profitable when they opened their doors.

The centers now serve a roster of the "bluest chip" companies in New York, Philadelphia, and Washington. But before she arrived at that lofty position, Diane Dennis went through a capitalization process that illustrates several key lessons. First, like many business owners, Diane started with her own capital—in this case, start-up capital of $87,000 in cash, additional money from a few other partners, and sweat equity.

As the business got under way, additional capital was needed, which meant a trip to the bank. Diane's husband, Warren Dennis, is one of the premiere attorney experts in the country on the workings of the Equal Credit Opportunity Act, so Warren wasn't surprised when the bank asked for his cosignature on the loan. The lender looked to the couple's house as backup equity for the loan, but the loan was given primarily on the basis of Warren's, not Diane's, income, because she had left her job. The Dennis family lives in Washington, D.C., a "common law" jurisdiction, so the creditor could look only to the income of the person who actually signed the loan—in this case, Warren Dennis. (Had the Dennises been residents of one of the nine community property states, Diane might, in theory, have received a business loan based on her husband's income.) Although the couple received the $250,000 needed for the business, Diane felt she could have qualified for at least $150,000 based on her real estate equity ownership. In any case, Diane recognized the importance of a supportive spouse whose commitment to the business augmented her own efforts. The couple did not have to put their home on the line—the bank granted an unsecured loan.

The center was profitable from the beginning, so their original loan has been paid off and new loans negotiated. But the banks are still requiring Dennis's husband to cosign her loans. The next financing step will be to achieve loans based on company performance alone. With the Lipton expansion model, that day may not be far away. They build a center, pay down the loan, and build a new center.

Before the company had expanded from Washington, D.C., to New York, they received a $1.5 million offer of equity capital for one-third of the company. Because the couple felt the company would be worth more after the New York expansion, they decided to turn that capital down, waiting to get the valuation up. The couple now is ready to seek expansion capital, and they expect to negotiate a more realistic evaluation. Even if no other capital is forthcoming, the "build them and open them" model will allow for slow, but indefinite, expansion.

When asked what's behind their success, Diane Dennis responds: "The company is driven by a desire to produce high-quality child care which meets kids' needs while returning dollars to the bottom line. Child care doesn't mean a whole lot to corporations in and of itself. But a company of three hundred or so people yields a return of $88,000 per year as a result of reduced absenteeism and a quick return from maternity leave." By designing a product she would use, Diane has cornered the backup child-care market, replacing the inefficient, informal patchwork of ad-hoc arrangements for absenteeism five years ago.

middle of such fiascoes as the recent savings and loan crisis. Despite your understanding the problem, your perspective will conflict with the banker's. From your point of view, you need your money and you need it now. From the lender's perspective, as much as the institution would like to earn

> "The system makes it very difficult for both the lender and the borrower to make or receive small loans, because you have to evaluate and provide the same documentation on a $50,000 loan as for a $2 million one."
>
> —*Interview with Barbara Davis Blum, chairwoman and CEO, The Abigail Adams National Bancorp, Inc.*

interest by loaning money to you, the officers are required to jump through regulatory hoops—for everyone. But don't forget that people can use "regulatory necessity" as a convenient excuse for discrimination.

In general, the list of what you'll need for *any* business loan, at a minimum, includes:

- Company profit and loss statements, if applicable, and financial projections. Start-ups would not yet have profit and loss statements, which show the company's historical income and expenses.

PAPERWORK TIP

If, like some entrepreneurs, you have been moving so fast that your paperwork house isn't in order, including the timely filing of your tax returns, now is the time to get things straight. Without up-to-date, written documentation, you're limiting your capital to the most expensive (credit cards) or informal (family and friends) sources.

- Your personal financial statement. If you don't have a financial statement, the bank will provide you a form, much like a home mortgage application or any longer credit application.
- Unless you are well known to the lender, a business plan, including background on the principals. If you've done business with the bank for several years, an informal letter about the direction of your ongoing or proposed business may suffice.
- A list of business debt, aged accounts receivable, and accounts payable.
- Personal and business tax returns for the past three years.
- Copy of property lease, if applicable.
- Any pertinent company contracts or agreements.
- Any other documentation you can provide that shows the lender where the money for repayment will come from, especially in the event your cash-flow projections don't materialize as planned.

The list is the same for virtually any kind of commercial bank loan. Some bankers have found women are not prepared for the informational requests loan officers make. Be able to provide the information above and recognize that a request by your banker for the personal information is standard; even though you are seeking a commercial loan, the bank is also betting on you. Be prepared.

THE EQUAL CREDIT OPPORTUNITY ACT AND BUSINESS CREDIT

Since the 1974 passage of the federal Equal Credit Opportunity Act (ECOA), women-owned businesses have increased eight-fold. What are the basic provisions of the Act? How did the Act open the door to increased business financing? What changes are needed to meet today's business environment?

THE ORIGINAL ECOA PROVISIONS

Upon passage of the equal credit act, discrimination in lending was outlawed on the basis of sex and marital status. Until passage, creditors routinely denied women credit on the basis that their decisions represented "sound business practice."

Shored up by the changing social climate and attitudes toward women and work on one hand and the Federal Reserve Board's Regulation B, or "Reg B," the enforcing provision of the Act ordinary, blatant refusal to deny women credit on the basis of gender changed fairly quickly. With marital status, the picture was more complicated because of the complications of marital property law as it varied among the states. In the 41 separate property states, based on English common law, creditors could not ask a person's marital status, although they could determine if a mortgaged property was likely to have other title claimants, such as a spouse. In the nine community states, based upon Spanish and Napoleonic legal systems, spouses could commit each other's earnings, depending upon the state, so creditors could ask marital status and even the non-labor force participant has a right to commit the other's earnings for some credit purposes.

Marital transitions continued to present problems, as they do today, as when a widow finds herself without credit after years of supporting a card or mortgage without her name on it. Such denial, without further investigation on the part of the creditor, remains illegal, but in practice women encounter it even in the 90s.

In addition to these provisions, for the first time the ECOA and Reg. B required that creditors provide timely application processing (rather than "losing" a questionable application) with legally mandated reasons for the denial.

With this arsenal of rights in hand, women started businesses with consumer credit. Since in many banks, small business loans are handled under consumer divisions, these regulations applied. As long as women applied for $100,000 or less, business credit informally fell under the consumer credit guidelines.

THE BUSINESS CREDIT DIFFERENCE

During the initial Senate passage of ECOA in 1973, the intention of the sponsors as expressed in Committee mark-up and reports, was that business credit would be fully covered by the Act. But in drafting Reg. B, business credit was accorded different procedures.

Getting turned down. While consumer credit applicants must receive their adverse action notice in writing, business loan applicants may receive oral notification instead. While a legitimate reason must be on file with the institution, being given a "no" over the phone can prove embarrassing and thwart further pressure from the applicant.

Record keeping. While consumer credit records must be kept for 25 months, business loans records only stay on file for 12. The Federal Reserve Board warns, "a woman business owner has to be more on the ball. If she thinks she's been discriminated against, she should take quick action."

The reality is that in the pressure of starting and keeping businesses alive, a business woman denied credit is more likely to shop elsewhere than seek formal redress.

SOLUTIONS FOR EQUAL CREDIT ACCESS

The problem of women's access to business credit runs deeper than the issues raised here. In addition to the technical aspects, an underlying problem is the change in the credit granting system itself in the last two decades as a result of computer centralization of records. With increased creditor skittishness, a broader marketplace on which to place capital, and tighter record-keeping, many women who need modest to mid-sized loans find they've been turned down for a couple of "30-day late" entries in their credit records. Because of past enforcement procedures, including limited data gathering, it's hard to track comparisons of the treatment of women and men in this regard.

In addition, well-meaning women's business advocates who have forgotten the meaning of "leg loans"—the antediluvian term for loans given to good-looking women—now are promoting "character loans" for women whose records are scant but who look like good entrepreneurial prospects.

The problem with all these efforts is that subjective factors can quickly be turned against an entrepreneur who doesn't exactly fit the model, while stringent score-keeping, as with the 30-day-late denial, may not screen correctly for entrepreneurial potential.

More thinking must be done on how to revamp the credit system to meet today's changed computer environment where there's no room for minor mistakes. New predictive scores need to be developed by banks, business and government lenders, and credit card companies that take the changed technology and business practices into account. In the meantime, the SBA's business loan programs provide the best alternative for women who cannot qualify for traditional business credit.

Five Rules for Smart Banking

Time and again, experts cite a lack of understanding by women of the banking process as a primary reason for women's unequal access to institutional capital. Preparation before you apply for a loan is critical to improving your chances for financing success.

1. Know your banker before you need to get a loan.

The key to dealing with banks is to establish a strong banking relationship. Being on a first-name basis with a friendly banker who has seniority is as good as gold. Even if the banker

> "If you need help, I'm much more likely to go further in accommodating you if I know you."
>
> —*Cellie Taafe, banker*

cannot give you the loan you want now, eventually, by working with the same person, you'll reach a point where your track record is well known to the banker. At that point, you'll have your financial backer.

Fortunately, the banking industry has changed since twenty-plus years ago, before the Equal Credit Opportunity Act, when lenders made "leg loans" to attractive women. Today, as in other areas of business life, smart women look for other smart women. Banking is one of the places where your comfort zone increases exponentially if you are able to present your business to another professional woman.

Whenever you open a new account, always make an appointment and meet with the branch manager or top official in the bank prior to opening the account. Be sure that you go down the chain of command from the beginning. Later, when you need special attention—instant credit for a large customer check or a temporary overdraft—the manager will have to make the decision. Management's knowing you from day one will work to your advantage.

2. Choose the right bank for you, depending on your own needs.

> **CREATIVE BANKING**
>
> In 1993, Athena Ubok read in the *Los Angeles Times* that several downtown Korean banks were not making enough loans to minorities after the L.A. riots. So she made it a point to apply for loans in Koreatown, Los Angeles. As a first-generation Hispanic-American, she quickly received a loan that enabled her to open Cafe Caribe.
>
> Source: *Interview with Athena Ubok, Los Angeles, May 1995.*

Although you are limited in your banking choices by location, you should look for a bank that will give you the service you need. If your loan needs will be moderate rather than in the million-dollar-plus level and you will rarely require interstate or international assistance, you can avoid using a conglomerate. Choose a community or smaller "boutique" bank that caters to clientele who relish personalized service. Most importantly, if you plan to get a loan guaranteed by the Small Business Administration (SBA), make sure the bank you select works with the SBA.

Many banks offer convenient services that help time-pressured entrepreneurs. Some banks will provide payroll services that work directly with your checking account. Other banks, in addition to night-drop service, actually pick up deposits from your office. In larger banks, such services are usually located in "high net worth" departments, where these and other special services are aimed at upscale customers.

> In 1990, two thirds of women applying for start-up business loans were required to have their husbands cosign for the loan.
>
> Source: *Center for Policy Alternatives.*

You can become a "preferred customer"—with all the conveniences and courtesies—by getting to know your banker, regardless of the size of your account. As you start out, this personal attention means a great deal.

3. Build a strong profile as a good bank customer.

If you want to make the best impression at your bank, the first step is elementary: Put your money in it. Even though this point seems obvious, you'd be surprised at the number of people who don't put their money into a bank from whom they expect to receive a bank loan.

If possible, have a major feeder account that you put all your money into, even if you later disburse it to other accounts, such as the one you use for your own personal expenses. By creating a steady, visible stream of income in your bank records, you're establishing an image with the bank.

If you're running tight and fear that a check might bounce, call your bank officer *beforehand* and let her know the details of when you're expecting specific income to cover the overdraft. Most banks can provide a short amount of overdraft protection (even if you don't have formal overdraft protection) if they know your income schedule.

> 4. *Be familiar with the new products in the financial marketplace, especially those designed for businesses.*

The banker's product is customer service, not money. For small businesses, offerings such as payroll services and payroll tax deposits can save a mountain of paperwork for a minimum in fees. And if your business capital amounts to enough to warrant it, be sure to put your funds into an interest-bearing cash management account.

As a business owner, you'll want to set up retirement accounts for yourself and your employees as soon as possible. Your banker can help you set up these accounts as well.

Banks also offer debit cards which provide the convenience of a credit card without the temptation. Since a

> Despite the importance of savings in strengthening the economy, only 15 percent of small businesses in 1995 had pension plans.
>
> *Source: White House Conference on Small Business.*

debit card directly accesses your checking account when used, it prevents you from overextending your credit. This service is ideal for tracking business travel and entertainment expenses.

> 5. *If you get into a dispute with your banker, resolve it quickly.*

The most common problems arise when a customer or the bank makes an error on a deposit and the problem snowballs. Checks bounce, worries rise, and both banker and customer get caught up in a "who's right" battle. Fax a letter to the bank outlining what went wrong and why. Don't let incidents slide without going on record, because banks routinely flag "problem accounts." Maintaining accurate records and written correspondence will help overcome these negative flags should you need special treatment in the future.

Why Women Have Trouble Getting Loans

Women clearly have always had difficulty getting bank loans for their ventures. The following are some reasons why female entrepreneurs have been denied credit.

- Perception of risk in lending to start-ups in general. Since women are starting businesses in record numbers, by definition, a large number of women-led businesses are less attractive to lenders.
- Women still face prejudice. Only two decades have passed since credit became widely available to women.

> Ironically, the inability to obtain credit has helped women during recessionary times because companies without debt are not burdened by interest payments. Of course, the opposite is true for women forced to finance their companies with high-interest credit-card debt.

- Because of a lack of experience and mentoring for women, some bankers allege that women are unprepared when meeting with loan officers.
- In tight markets, lenders go with the tried and true; in other words, men.
- Women's incomes are lower than men's prior to starting businesses.
- Women may not be perceived as entrepreneurs as a class of individuals.
- Women may tend to start smaller businesses. From the lender's perspective, it's as hard to get a $50,000 loan as a $500,000 loan, because the documentation for each is the same. It's more cost effective for the lender to service one $500,000 loan than ten $50,000 loans.
- Women may not present as much collateral as men because their asset bases are smaller. Also, women tend to start service-, not asset-based, businesses.

> "70 percent of women business owners bankrolled the start-up and the expansion phases of their businesses with personal credit cards or loans from family or friends because they couldn't get a bank loan."
>
> —Betsy Myers, assistant deputy to the president

Credit Cards

Credit cards, although one of the most frequently used sources of start-up capital for women, should be used with great care. Using credit cards for start-up capital is dangerous for two reasons: If something goes wrong and you need cash for personal expenses, you'll have no fall-back position; and the exorbitant interest rates charged by credit-card companies will quickly burden your company's cash flow.

> Women are three times as likely as men to use personal credit cards to start a business.
>
> Source: Center for Policy Alternatives.

Also, in general, credit-card collections are much tougher and much less negotiable than commercial loans. If you get into a tight spot, once a bank has backed you, it is likely to stick with you for as long as it can. By contrast, being even sixty days behind on a credit card can put a black mark on your credit record. In addition, interest rates on credit cards also run much higher than commercial loans, so you'll pay more for less favorable credit.

Of course, there are advantages to using credit cards, most notably their ease of access. Many successful businesses have been started on a few simple cash advances. Some female advocates even promote the use of credit cards to get your business off the ground, should all else fail, because most women with a strong commitment and concept have survived in their ventures despite the high credit-card payments and interest. Nonetheless, credit cards should be used only with caution.

TYPES AND SOURCES OF FINANCING*

Types of Short-Term Financing

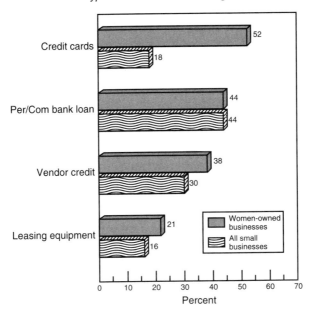

Types of Long-Term Financing

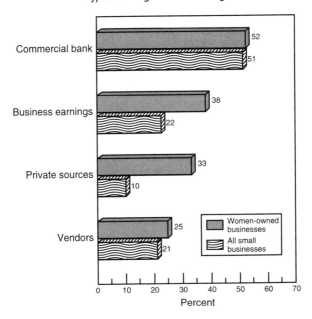

*Multiple responses allowed

Source: NWBC 1994 Report to President, p. 4.

Remember that the process of searching for financing, though often frustrating, will also strengthen your plans and your network. Don't use credit cards just because they appear to be the easiest way to start; they're not.

Home Refinancing

Home refinancing represents the very worst choice for start-up business credit. Your home usually represents your greatest equity. If you use it to start your business, you can lose your home and still not be assured of business success.

The home is particularly vulnerable because a home loan is secured by the property itself. The lender can take your home if you don't make your payments.

> The number of women using credit cards, home refinancing, and noncommercial loans to finance their businesses tripled from 1982 to 1987.
>
> *Source: U.S. Census Bureau Economic Census of Women-Owned Businesses, 1987.*

Homes are often the linchpin of a comfortable retirement. Without a home, it's very hard to secure your retirement. For women, losing a home presents an even more devastating picture than for men. Women tend to rely on social security alone, without the benefit of other pension funds, and on average, women outlive men. Before you place your home at risk, think long and hard.

Despite the dangers, determined entrepreneurs risk their dwellings for their dreams every year. If you are planning to put your home at risk to start your business, consider waiting until you can save the funds for start-up. If you can't save enough, then recognize how hard it will be to resave your home equity.

Resources and References

Your best resource for loan information is your community banker. Equipped with your new knowledge of the banking process, you can intelligently inquire about small business services and loans at your local bank.

Emily Card's *Staying Solvent: A Comprehensive Guide to Equal Credit for Women* (New York: Holt, Rinehart and Winston, 1985) explains how to obtain credit and how to utilize the protection of credit laws.

CHAPTER 3

Private Sources of Capital

To many, the world of small business and entrepreneurship is defined by one thing: venture capital. Today, the world of venture capital is best described as a search for the next Apple Computer or Federal Express. The culture is high-tech, ultrahigh growth, and typically high testosterone.

For obvious reasons, women have taken a backseat. The small service businesses women tend to start are not attractive to impatient venture capitalists hooked on techno-hits; there are very few female venture capitalists;

> *Venture capital* defined: The pool of risk funds available to start or expand a small company. Institutional and private investors offer money and management aid in exchange for an ownership position in a new firm.

and women are not proven quantities as high-risk, high-growth entrepreneurs. Nonetheless, each of these barriers is beginning to be overcome. Women are entering more varied industries. Though their numbers are still minuscule, female venture capitalists and women-owned venture capital firms are taking root. And the number of successful women-owned businesses continues to increase. As a result, you can now seriously consider private venture capital investment as a potential source of capital for your business.

Private Investors

The ideal investor—like the ideal mate—is hard to come by. The ideal for most is someone with plenty of money who respects you and your ideas, gives you free reign of the venture, shares your values, and offers advice only when appropriate.

The reality often stands in sharp contrast to the ideal. An investor may be a dilettante who wants to micromanage your every move because she has nothing else to do with her time. You may end up thinking, "Why didn't this woman go into business herself if she knew so much?" Or the investor may know nothing about your business but a lot about another business that doesn't mesh with yours. He insists on giving you advice anyway. Even if the investor knows your business, she may be completely supportive—or second-guess every decision you make.

On the other hand, the investor may be a wonderful part of the management advisory team, providing not only capital but expertise. Others want to be silent partners and hear from you infrequently, sometimes too infrequently. Such an arrangement can be dangerous if you face a downturn because the investor won't be prepared to supply needed additional capital.

Remember that it is often difficult to take an investment without taking along the investor. Once he's in your bed, it may be even harder to get the investor out than it was to get him in.

What to Look for in an Individual Investor

When searching for a private investor, first determine whether you want someone who is active or passive. Second, try to be sure the investor you find agrees with your basic values and operating style. You and your investor will go through tough times together—count on it. As in a marriage, little differences can turn into big irritants.

As a woman business owner, you'll have particular needs that your investor must acknowledge and validate. For example, time constraints around children can't be brushed aside. Housekeeping support services may be essential. Don't expect the investor to underwrite a lavish personal life-style. By contrast, if your potential money source frowns in disapproval when you need to cut a meeting short to pick up the kids, then you're headed for trouble.

Third, check out the investor's personality. You don't want a moody, capricious, or unreliable investor. You need emotional maturity and steadfastness from your financial partners.

> 1,260,400 American households reported a net worth of over $1 million in 1989.
>
> Source: Internal Revenue Service, Statistics of Income Division.

Fourth, be sure that you both agree on how the investor will exit or complete his or her investment in your business. While the goal of venture capitalists is often to take the company public, individual investors don't necessarily expect this conclusion. Work out the exit strategy in advance, including repayment plans that will allow you to keep the business private, if that's your preference.

Understanding the Investor's Perspective

When people put their capital at risk in a new business (or any other high-risk investment), they put their livelihood on the line. In your

FROM THE GOLDEN DOOR TO EUREKA COMMUNI-TIES, DEBORAH SZEKELEY'S BUSINESS IS CHANGE

While it's hard to recall now, in the not-distant past, American was a meat and pota-toes country, and vegetarians and health foods were reserved for the very eccentric. While many forces combined to change the way Americans address health issues, it's not a stretch of the truth to say that Deborah Szekeley was the moving force behind bringing European-style health spas to this continent and health food diets to Idaho kitchens.

Deborah's story started in 1939 when as a 17-year old girl she set out with Profes-sor Szekeley, a scholar and "natural-living experimenter," to found a new life-style for themselves. What they began as a camp in the northern Mexican village of Tecate became Rancho La Puerta, the ranch of the door. The door that was opened over the ensuring years introduced many Americans to a mixture of philosophy, vegetarian cui-sine, sun-air-water baths, whole grain foods, organic vegetables, outdoor exercise, and meditation. In short, most of what we now know today to be a healthy life-style, endorsed not just by "health nuts" but by the medical establishment.

From Rancho La Puerta, Deborah Szekeley later realized a dream of opening a lux-ury spa. Named the Golden Door, the private, secluded, up-scale equivalent of the orig-inal door was added in 1958 to cater to affluent opinion makers who needed an ulti-mate break. Since its founding, the Golden Door has been a temporary home to media, movie, business, and political celebrities.

How did the 17-year-old girl and the professor capitalize such exotic businesses? By going slowly. Deborah says the professor's saying, "Only as far as the blanket will spread," carried her through each stage of expansion. By that, Deborah means that she doesn't go out on limbs and take risks, at least as far as her capital is concerned. While her business would be deemed high-risk by most venture capitalists, her approach is conservative.

Being the wise woman that she is Deborah Szekeley also knew when to let her mature business pass into the hands of the next generation. Rather than hanging on to the reins, Deborah turned the business management over to her son, Alex, and she turned her own attention first to government service and then to giving back to the larger community.

Taking techniques she learned as the director of the Inter-American Foundation, an agency that seeks to assist in community development abroad, Deborah reimported the lessons and applies them to communities around the United States. To see Debo-rah Szekeley today is to see a woman with a successful entrepreneurial career behind her who has now turned her talents and her money toward helping people in inner cities by providing their community leadership with professional support and training.

Deborah Szekeley is living the ultimate entrepreneur's dream—she's turning her capital to help other 17-year-olds with dreams of their own.

For more on Eureka Communities write 1601 Connecticut Avenue, N.W., Suite 802, Washington, D.C.; (202) 332-2070; fax: (202) 332-0090.

mind, the $20,000 you need may appear to be an inconsequential investment for a millionaire. From the perspective of an investor with a net worth of $1 million, the loss of $20,000 represents the loss of 2 percent of her income base, the money on which interest can be earned. Were the millionaire to risk $100,000 and lose it, that's 10 per-cent of her net worth. Losing 10 percent of your net worth hurts, no matter how large the total. Because of the investment risk inherent in new ventures, investors expect both a degree of control and a substantial piece of the action.

Inherited-wealth investors and entrepreneurial investors tend to diverge in their perspectives. Inherited-wealth investors often have all the time in the world to make an investment decision, and they have one overriding objective: not to lose any money. Often the inherited-wealth investor is risk-averse because if the investment is lost, the investor may not possess the necessary skills to replace the lost funds. By contrast, the self-made entrepreneurial investor may be willing to take more risks because he is more confident that the money can be replaced.

> **WEALTH GEOGRAPHY**
>
> People with gross assets over $600,000 and total net worth under $10 million live in the following places:
>
> | | |
> |---|---|
> | CA: | 2,059,200 |
> | NY: | 1,025,800 |
> | FL: | 798,000 |
> | TX: | 577,900 |
> | NJ: | 526,500 |
> | IL: | 481,100 |
> | MA: | 341,700 |
>
> Source: Internal Revenue Service, Statistics of Income Division.

On the other hand, inherited-wealth investors often have more money to invest. Given a fortune of, say, $10 million, the loss of $100,000 wouldn't mean so much. Also, while the experience of a self-made investor can be a valuable asset to business start-up, the entrepreneur may get more management advice than bargained for. The inherited-wealth investor who wants to put money in and stay out of the way can be ideal. But watch out for the dilettante inherited-wealth investor who combines the worst of both worlds, meddling in management with no business knowledge and a fear of risk.

Contrary to professional venturists, both the wealthy and entrepreneurial private investor ordinarily don't seek the same short-term level of returns that the venture capitalist expects. Typically, individual investors are involved in fewer deals and expect relatively less risk but are willing to support the venture over a longer period of time. The venture capitalist is more like a roulette player, placing chips on the table with the expectation that one in ten deals will pay off handsomely, carrying the risk and the profit of the other nine.

Lead Investors

Individual investors are like sheep. They want to invest with other investors, especially *lead investors* who have a track record of success and are capable of putting together a group of investors who will stay in a deal. These lead investors come in two types. Some have made substantial money in a particular area and now lead other investors in that industry. Other lead investors operate on a full-time basis and have enjoyed investment success in a number of fields.

One critical problem facing women is the dearth of female lead investors. Very few women stand out in the investment community as successful lead investors—or for that matter, as any kind of investors.

For an entrepreneur, selling to a lead investor is like striking gold. If you can identify a lead investor in your field and sell that person on your business, you'll be in an excellent position to meet your funding requirements through private sources of capital.

Finding the Individual Investor

Individual investors represent a vital and underutilized source of capital, especially start-up capital for larger ventures. As the venture grows, banks and venture capital firms will be more receptive to your needs. Until then, you need to know where to find these individual investors.

ANGEL NETWORKS

In order to facilitate the flow of venture deals to private investors, groups of individual investors known as *angel networks* have sprung up around the country. Some people see these angel networks themselves as the source of capital, but this is incorrect. Securities laws prevent these networks from investing directly. Rather, the angel networks exist to find and screen potential venture capital deals for their members, the individual investors.

If you have a chance to present your business plan before an angel network, you can connect with individual investors in the most opportune way. You will be marketing your venture to a target audience of financiers. The investors will be primed to consider new investment opportunities and your presentation will be considered seriously.

> The term *angel*, often used to describe individual investors, comes from Broadway, where traditionally, angels have stepped forward to fund the production of shows. Angels are characterized by a kind of distant magic.

To get your venture in front of the angel network, your deal usually has to go through a screening process. The deal flow screening process is meant to select promising opportunities to be presented to the network's members. Angel networks usually respond to midrange deals between $100,000 and $1 million, with investment units of $25,000 to $250,000, too large for friends and family and often too small or too early for venture capital firms.

The selection committees for these networks try to be rational in their appraisals, yet they inevitably turn to the factors that guide all of us in our daily lives. Do we know this person? What do we know about her? Is the word on the street that this deal is hot?

During the selection process, the entrepreneur and her team of advisors and managers account for about 50 percent of the decision. The other half depends on the business plan, the financial projections, and whether the deal fits the investor group's stated profile of interests. The importance of the personality of the entrepreneur cannot be overstated. Even though the investors are buying a piece of the company, they are betting on you, the individual entrepreneur.

Keep that point in mind. As you work toward building your business, your total life experience will come into play. Have you had success in this business? Have you had success in a related business? Do you exhibit the kind of drive and determination that will carry you and your business through the inevitable ups and downs of entrepreneurial life? Here, being Ms. Goody Two-Shoes isn't important; demonstrating that you can take the heat is.

While it's helpful to be known by members of the network, don't worry if you're a new kid on the block. If you are not personally known to the investors, the selection committee will usually contact people who know you and your field.

One such network, the Investors' Circle, welcomes prospectuses from women entrepreneurs. If you want to know more about the Investors' Circle and its offspring, contact Capital Missions Company, 31W007 N. Avenue, Ste. 101, West Chicago, IL 60185. Phone 708-876-1101.

FAMILY OFFICES

Most of us don't even know what a family office is, but inherited-wealth families do. Old fortunes with a long history of inheritance manage their money through family offices. These offices are hard to locate; however, if you meet a wealthy person you might inquire whether they have a family office. If so, you can forward a copy of your business proposal there for consideration by the family office manager. These managers are paid to advise on investment directions and to screen such proposals; therefore, it's perfectly proper to make such a request. By contrast, you wouldn't want to meet a wealthy heir and immediately ask if she were interested in investing in your business.

Venture Capitalists—Call Them VCs for Short

The venture capital (VC) marketplace emerged during the Vietnam War era, and to many, venture capitalists and VC firms still resemble the other VCs, the Vietcong. VCs spend an enormous amount of time flying around the country employing guerrilla tactics to locate the one hit out of hundreds of potential new venture deals they see each year.

The venture capital field involves high pressure, long hours, and 100 percent dedication to career. Competition

> "The whole idea of traditional venture capital is to invest in the stock of a young company for as little as possible and to sell it for as much as possible while owning it for as short a time as possible."
>
> —Bruce Blechman and Jay Conrad Levinson, Guerrilla Financing (Boston: Houghton Mifflin, 1991), p. 164

for good deals is stiff. Out of thousands of possible investments, the number of clear-cut winners is in the teens.

VCs are some of the busiest and most sought-after people in the business world. Because of the high risk involved and their negotiating leverage, VCs work under tremendous pressure. They can often appear terse to the point of brusqueness. If you are lucky enough to land a meeting with a venture capital investor, don't take their manners (or lack thereof) personally. Be prepared with sound bites rather than paragraphs when you begin your discussion. If the VCs want more, they'll ask. Once you have made the contact, continue patient but dedicated follow-up.

> A woman seeking capital actually sent this message only two days after she mailed her proposal: "You promised me you'd call back. Why haven't I heard from you?" Be persistent, but be patient and polite.

Many people shy away from venture money because they've heard tales of the high degree of control and ownership imposed by venturists. The trade-off: a business adequately capitalized and expertly advised. Decide your preference—all of a small pie or a small piece of a big pie. Remember, if you are able to make a VC deal, you've probably got a company that's going places. That stamp of legitimacy can carry you a long way with your own audience—the marketplace, customers, suppliers, bankers, and other investors. Don't turn up your nose at venture capital. But watch your step.

In general, venture capitalists look for early-stage or mezzanine companies in high-growth glamour industries such as electronics, computer hardware, medical devices, and other technology-driven opportunities. Other kinds of companies do get venture capital infusions, particularly by regional or industry-focused venture capital firms. Some venture capitalists, such as members of the Investor's Circle, have even focused on nontraditional, socially responsible venture investments, including women- and minority-owned businesses.

Venture Capital Deal Structures

When it comes to capital structure, VCs like to have their cake and eat it too. Venture capitalists want debt to get paid back first if the company fails and equity to share in the profits if the company succeeds.

The result: VCs prefer to invest in convertible preferred stock or debentures. This kind of investment ensures that the venture capitalist will be repaid before other investors *and*, if the company is doing well, that the venture capitalist can get a healthy share of the profits. In general, VCs

> "The key to weathering the venture capital process is to put the transaction in perspective. When it's all over, your young and not particularly bankable company will have a large sum of cash to put to work."
>
> —Harvard Business Review, *March–April 1987*, *p. 24*

take a 40 to 60 percent share of the company in return for their investment.

Many venture capitalists are infamous for also taking warrants or coupons that, in essence, give the VC control of the company should the venture sour. By contrast, other venture capitalists start out in control and give the entrepreneur warrants or coupons that are redeemable to regain control of the company only when the venture is successful. Of course, lawyers often get involved to resolve disputes over whether or not the venture is sufficiently successful or unsuccessful for control of the company to shift.

Regardless of the structure, venture capitalists are demanding in their definition of success. VCs expect extremely high returns, as high as 70 percent compounded annual returns, and they expect a venture to reach high profitability within three to five years. In this sense, VCs are home-run hitters, preferring to repeatedly strike out in hopes of finding one extremely successful venture.

Given all the warnings and conditions, you may wonder whether to proceed. The decision will involve important considerations on your part that should not be minimized. Make sure that you have a personality and mind-set that can live within the limits that the involvement of venture capitalists will impose. If you left your job because you wanted to control your own day-to-day life, then don't trade off your authority for money.

Where the VCs Hang Out

From the description of VCs, you might think you'd find them in the jungle, hiding behind palm fronds with vines hanging from their helmets. In actuality, VCs look pretty normal, except for the dark circles under their eyes. The following locations are where you will find venture capitalists.

VENTURE FIRMS

VC firms are ongoing enterprises managed by experienced venture capitalists. The venture capital firm raises funds employing primarily two methods: The firm sells either stock or partnership interests in individual funds that invest a specified amount of capital over a specified period of time in an approximate number of new ventures. Sometimes VC firms specialize in a specific region or industry. Other times the funds are earmarked for a specific investment type, such as women-owned ventures.

In either case, investors fail or succeed in relation to the aggregate of venture investments made. In other words, the investments are cross-collateralized. If one of seven venture investments is extremely

**NEW COMMITMENTS, DISBURSEMENTS, AND TOTAL CAPITAL POOL OF THE
VENTURE CAPITAL INDUSTRY.**

Year	New Commitments to Venture Capital Firms	Disbursements to Funded Companies (billions of dollars)	Number of Funded Companies	Total Investment Capital Pool At End of Year* (billions of dollars)
1993	2.5	1.7**	640**	
1992	2.5	2.54	1,207	31.1
1991	1.3	1.4	792	32.9
1990	1.8	2.3	1,176	36.0
1989	2.4	3.4	1,465	34.4
1988	2.9	3.8	1,530	31.1
1987	4.1	4.0	1,740	29.0
1986	3.3	3.2	1,512	24.1
1985	3.3	2.7	1,388	19.6
1984	4.2	2.7	1,410	16.3
1983	4.5	2.5	1,236	12.1
1982	1.7	1.4	828	6.7

*The capital pool at year end should equal the total pool at the end of the previous year plus new commitments, minus the amount of net withdrawal (or liquidation) from the funds. For 1983, an additional $600 million was identified that had not been included in the prior estimate.

**For the first half of 1993

NA = Not available.

Source: Venture Capital Journal, various issues, Capital Publishing Corporation.

successful, the VC firm may be profitable even if the other six ventures fail. In most cases, significant returns from a new VC firm or fund are not expected within the first five to seven years.

VENTURE FUNDS

Venture funds are set up for a limited period of time by either venture firms or individual venturists (fund managers) to invest in a group of companies.

Funds are generally targeted to specific types of investments. Some funds focus on growing areas, such as media and biotech firms. A few funds even have a socially responsible mandate, targeting minority-owned, women-owned, and environmentally sound ventures.

No discussion of venture capital leaders would be complete without acknowledging Patricia Cloherty's role as the first nationally visible woman venture capitalist. After holding high office at the SBA under President Carter, Cloherty went on to head her own firm, Patricof & Co. Ventures headquartered in New York City, with branches in key locations. Pat's as tough as they come—but with heart. She's often opened doors for women and stands as a model for the next generation of women VCs, many of whom are trying to organize informal networks of women VCs. It's no coincidence that Pat also served as president of the National Venture Capital Association.

SOLO VENTURE CAPITALISTS

As explained above, some individual investors operate as full-time, solo venture capitalists. Working alone, these guys—and they will be guys—can drive you nuts or make your company. They often want to replicate their success in another industry or use their self-made money to branch out, applying their management and entrepreneurial skills to make money in your industry. Solo venture capitalists can best be found through angel networks or at venture fairs, which are usually sponsored by such networks.

VENTURE ASSOCIATIONS

National and local venture associations provide directories of VC firms, VC funds, and individual venture capitalists. Some venture associations hold meetings of local venture capitalists that are open to networking visits.

VCs NATIONWIDE

National Venture Capital Association

National Association of Small Business Investment Companies (NASBIC)

National Association of Investment Companies (NAIC)

VENTURE FAIRS

Just as the county pulls together its best produce and livestock for the county fair, the venture marketplace puts some of its best deals on show at *venture fairs*. The annual cycle of venture fairs, produced both by associations and firms, offers businesspersons an opportunity to present start-up ideas to an assembled audience of investors. Because the buyers in the room know other buyers, word of mouth about hot deals quickly goes out from the venture fair into the venture capital world.

If you get an opportunity to present at a venture fair, make the best of it. Don't go until you are ready, complete with a professional presentation. At venture fairs the presentations include color slide shows, videos, product demonstrations, and product giveaways.

VENTURE FAIRS

Most venture fairs are regional, but some national venture fairs bring together entrepreneurs, private investors, and venture capitalists from around the nation, including Venture One, Private Equity Analyst, and The Investors' Circle.

One frustration of presenters at fairs is the expense of presenting, from registration fees to materials preparation. There is also a long lead time between presenting and getting the money. A successful process can take from six to eighteen months, including following up with all the leads, additional presentations, preparation of supplemental materials, site visits to your business, and negotiating the final deal. At any point, the deal can fall apart, leaving you disappointed and seemingly with no capital. Yet, when entrepreneurs go though this process, the experience prepares them to meet with other venturists. Sometimes, the VC community will hear the story of a near-success and, knowing the players, will step in to invest. Because the outcome is unpredictable, obtaining money from an individual venture firm must be approached simultaneously with preparing for fair-type presentations. In fact, the VC community is so small and so driven by word of mouth that by the time you get to the fair, it is often only a final testing ground to see how you take the heat.

Approaching the Venture Capitalist

The world of venture has been a world of men interested in high-tech, high-growth companies. If your undertaking involves putting

---

THE FIRST VC FUND AIMED AT WOMEN

Peggy Wyant, Blue Chip Opportunity Fund, Cincinnati

Blue Chip Venture is a $50 million venture capital fund founded by Jack Wyant, a committed venture capitalist with heart. The original fund focuses on high technology in the Cincinnati area, while its offshoot, the Blue Chip Opportunity Fund, is committed to funding women- and minority-owned businesses.

In an unusual model, Jack's wife Peggy Wyant conceived targeting women through a separate $15 million fund for women and minorities who are "underserved in the capital venture community." The Blue Chip Opportunity Fund will consider businesses at any stage in any area of the country. Wyant is proud that the Opportunity Fund, founded in 1991, is the first fund directed toward women.

Peggy Wyant, whose commitment to funding women-led businesses couldn't be clearer, provides an interesting perspective on why women don't get venture. "Women are harder to sort out. More businesses are being started; more are successful; and they're growing at a faster rate. But, up until recently, women have not been as risk-oriented, partly because in the past the capital has been not there for them. While the infusion of venture capital leads to a higher success rate, women are still not as ready as men to 'jump off the bridge.' From the venture capital point of view, women are not as responsive to faster growth opportunities." Peggy continues that she's seen people who wanted $250,000 but balked at taking a larger amount. In one case, she asked an entrepreneur, "What would you do if you had $2.5 million?" The woman's response was that she felt she couldn't raise that much. By contrast, men will ask for $5 million to $10 million, pitching that they're creating a billion-dollar company, when it's often obviously a wild dream.

Peggy says, "Women do their homework, make more conservative estimates, and fail to get the capital." One lesson here: Backers expect entrepreneurs to exaggerate; women's clearer picture of reality may work against them in getting venture backing, even though the same bent produces a better success rate on businesses that do get up and running.

Another key point: "Service businesses are not traditionally backable, but that's where America is moving." That is also where women-owned businesses are strongest. And Peggy believes venture capital will soon move in that direction.

day-care backup systems in place, as Lipton Child Care Centers is doing, going the traditional VC route may not make sense. Yet the venture business is becoming more open to new ideas. The demographics of change are simply too compelling to ignore. Venture capitalists recognize that media content, services, and women-owned businesses will dominate the small business landscape in the next century.

> Women-owned businesses documented receipts of $98.3 billion in 1982 and will generate over $1 trillion in revenue by the year 2000.
> *Source: National Women's Business Council.*

Whether you are working with venture capital firms, a commercial or association venture fair, or an angel network, deals for further investigation and commitment often are chosen by committee. Within a firm, the management or investment committee will normally make the selections. Within trade organizations or angel networks where deals flow and venture fairs are sponsored, a screening committee will make the cut.

Being known personally or through a positive reputation makes a world of difference at selection time. When people look good on paper but no one has ever heard of them, sometimes suspicion is actually generated. The selection committee members ask, "If she's so great, why don't I know her?"

Networking with the VC community in informal ways before you need the money can be advantageous. Having a powerful sponsor also helps. If you want support from a venture fund or you hope to present at a venture fair, knowing a lead member of the organization paves your way to at least getting a good hearing. The company you keep also makes a big difference. If your business boasts an illustrious advisory board, then people feel that you have both good contacts and good advice.

Negatives about a person can kill the deal, much like a sorority blackball. If you've had some business failures and rebounded, that's okay. But leaving behind a trail of negative experiences mounts up to a negative reputation.

Recognize that VCs tend to specialize. They prefer to do business in areas that they understand. Regardless of the potential of your venture, VCs typically adhere to their region or specialty and will not consider your plans if they fall outside that scope. Consequently, you should be knowledgeable about the venture capitalists you approach.

THE VENTURE CAPITAL MARKETPLACE TODAY

Like all markets, the venture capital market is cyclical. During some periods, available investment funds shrink, and predictions of doom abound. Around the corner, the market recovers and more money becomes available for investment than there are good deals.

Like other sectors of American business, the number of players continues to consolidate, meaning that the decisions fall to fewer and fewer people to make. This fact makes your approach all the more critical. Demonstrating you've done your homework carries you a great distance.

Venture firms have preferences for their investments. In order to make an informed approach, you need to learn the firms' profiles according to a number of preferences, including:

> **VC ROLLER COASTER**
>
> Over the years, VC firms have gone up and down in the amount of money they have been able to raise:
>
> 1985: $2.1 billion
> 1987: $3.6 billion
> 1989: $3.4 billion
> 1991: $1.4 billion
> 1993: $2.9 billion
> 1994: $4.3 billion
>
> Source: Glenn Riskin, "A Generation Gap in Venture Capital," New York Times, 25 May 1995, C1.

geographic region
stage of venture development
amount of capital required
type of capital required (start-up, acquisition)
industry
market niche
management
ownership

Using these criteria, prepare a target list of firms. Search first in your area, since that will make approaching them easier and less expensive. Also, look for women working on the management committee or as principals, since presumably there will be some interest in other women by female VCs.

MEETING THE VENTURE CAPITALIST

The best way to earn a meeting with a venture capitalist is through a *quality introduction*. Try to find a banker, lawyer, accountant, or other entrepreneur who has a contact with the firm. Get a listing of projects previously funded and see if you have pathways to the firm through their entrepreneurs' success. Although your

> "The perception that institutional venture capital is not a good arena for women becomes a self-fulfilling prophecy. Women with qualified investments need to be less timid about approaching venture capital firms. Venture capital is not as inaccessible as it might seem."
>
> —Sona Wang, partner, Inroads Capital

business plan is a required admission ticket to the VCs office, a meeting is required to open negotiations. In fact, one of the primary purposes of the business plan is to get a meeting with potential investors. Meetings are vital—very few plans submitted actually produce a face-to-face meeting, so if you get the opportunity, take your meeting with great seriousness. Be prepared to talk, without notes and with real authority, on the following topics:

    your current business progress to date
    when profits are expected to be returned
    your exit strategy (although this is rarely discussed with start-ups)

Also be ready to make a formal presentation. Don't be shocked if the venturist veers into his or her own agenda, quizzing you backward and forward about your ideas. Don't let this throw you off balance. It's a game, nothing more. Venture capitalists want to see if you can survive in any business situation that's thrown your way, including the one you're in right at that time. Hang tough. Your foot's in the door. Now wedge in your whole body, so to speak. If not now, when?

Resources and References

Because you can't find "Venture Capitalists" in the yellow pages, a bit of digging is required to locate this rich source of potential capital. Many resources are available to help you in your search.

The macro level of research starts with the overview of directories provided in *Directories in Print* (Detroit: Gale Research Inc., 1995), a rich resource. Use this book as a starting point if you have no idea what directories to consult.

Another resource that proves fruitful in searching for venture capital sources for women is *Business Organizations, Agencies, and Publications Directory: A Guide to Approximately 30,000 New and Established Organizations, Agencies, and Publications Concerned with International and U.S. Business, Trade, and Industry* (Detroit: Gale Research Inc., 1993). This directory includes organizations, government agencies, research libraries, publications, and information services. From market research to an on-line service to complement your area of business activity— you can find these listed here. Women- and minority-owned business resources, newsletters, and organizations appear in the index. Much of the information is geographically organized, so you can find what you need in your local area.

The major listing of venture capital firms in the United States is *Pratt's Guide to Venture Capital Sources* (Wellesly Hills, MA: Capital Publishing, 1995). The listings are by state and firm. The information in the directory may be a little disconcerting. When looking through California venture capital firms, in the section from A to C, covering several pages, we found only three women listed under "management" or "who to contact," and none listed as the principal venture capitalists—definitely a male club. Consequently, any woman seeking venture capital is well advised to call or write the women VCs in her area. As a starting point, the women listed in Pratt's will provide you access to a small, tight-knit, and cliquish community. Look in Pratt's or any other VC directory and scan the lists for women. (And see the appendix for our listing of female venture capitalists interested in other women as investment opportunities.)

A. David Silver's *The Venture Capital Sourcebook* (Chicago: Irwin Professional Publishers, 1994) is an excellent reference book for locating venture capitalists. The book also contains information to help prepare you to meet venture capitalists. David Gladstone's *Venture Capital Handbook* (Englewood Cliffs, NJ: Prentice Hall, 1988) similarly discusses the world of venture capital.

Local venture capital associations typically organize venture capital breakfasts and other networking events. You can contact your local Chamber of Commerce to find them. You can also find a list of scheduled local venture capital forums and venture fairs in *Venture Capital Journal* each month.

To reach Blue Chip Opportunity Fund, write Blue Chip Venture Company, 2000 PNC Center, 201 E. 5th Street, Cincinnati, OH 45202. Phone 513-723-2300; fax 513-723-2306.

VENTURE CAPITAL ORGANIZATIONS

National Venture Capital Association, 1655 North Fort Myer Drive, Ste. 700, Arlington, VA 22209. Select group of VCs.

National Association of Small Business Investment Companies (NASBIC), P.O. Box 2039, Merrifield, VA 22116. Phone 703-683-1601; fax 703-683-1605. For SBICs.

National Association of Investment Companies (NAIC), 1111 14th Street, NW, Washington, DC 20005. Phone 202-289-4336. For MESBICS.

International Venture Capital Institute, P.O. Box 1333, Stamford, CT 06904. Phone 203-323-3143; fax 203-359-5858. Publications include Directory of Business Incubators, Directory of Venture Capital Seed and Early Stage Funds.

CHAPTER 4

Government Sources
of Capital

For a businessperson, voluntarily coming into contact with the government might seem the last place to go for capital. Most of us, if we deal with the government at all, deal in negatives: the IRS, OSHA, licenses, and regulations.

Yet surprisingly, the government can be an extremely productive avenue to capital. Federal loans, small business investment corporations, and procurement contracts represent three potential sources of debt capital, equity capital, and business activity. The government is also the primary place to bring about change in laws and policies affecting women business owners. Despite the bureaucracy involved, you may want to consider tackling the government in your quest for capital.

Depending on your political point of view, you may think that government has no business mixing with business. Perhaps you want nothing to do with government-guaranteed loans because you don't want the extra paperwork or you don't want to validate the government's involvement in the private sector by partici-

FEDERAL PROCUREMENT AND WOMEN-LED BUSINESSES
▪ $174.5 billion per year is spent on goods and services by the federal government.
▪ $4.9 billion is awarded to women-led businesses.
Source: Small Business Administration, fiscal year 1994.

pating in the federal small business programs yourself. But like it or not, the government spends money. Daily the government buys products and services from scores of businesspeople. If your business fits the government's purchasing requirements, you could be among the government suppliers who have a steady customer with a perfect record of paying its bills.

Government legislation—from tax codes to occupational safety regulations to affirmative action policies (or lack of them)—creates the environment in which businesses operate. Although policies and programs are subject to change with shifting political trends, the government has sought to support small business, especially focusing on assistance to women and minorities.

In this chapter and the next, we'll look at some of the most active programs. Don't stop with what we can provide here. Throughout the federal government, the enterprising entrepreneur can locate opportunities—loans, technical assistance, and contracts. Our objective is to provide you a map to key locations. Your treasure hunt may turn up other agencies and projects that fit your profile as well.

Getting Loans from the Government

Federal loan programs for small business are conducted almost exclusively through the Small Business Administration (SBA). While the SBA provides very few direct grants or loans, the agency is the major underwriter of business loans in the United States through the SBA's guaranteed loan programs. SBA loans are important to business-people because, given the identical set of facts, a person can obtain an SBA loan more easily than a similar commercial loan. Because of its sensitivity to the needs of women-owned businesses, the Small Business Administration has become one of the best sources of loan guarantees for women-owned businesses.

The SBA has taken steps to become more accessible to entrepreneurs. The SBA can be reached at U.S. Small Business Administration, 409 Third Street, S.W., Washington, DC 20416. Phone (SBA Answer Desk) 800-8-ASK-SBA. The SBA Online can be reached by phone at 800-697-4636, through the SBA's home page at http://wwwsbaon line.sba.gov, or through networkMCI's website at http://www. mci.com. For your local SBA office, check your telephone directory under "U.S. Government."

SBA Loan Programs

The primary financial opportunity within the SBA itself is its loan guarantee programs. The SBA does not directly give most of its loans; rather, the SBA guarantees loans on behalf of the small business applicant much as a cosigner would. Like a traditional bank loan, the participating banks actually give the loans and the entrepreneurs are expected to repay the loans themselves.

The loans are attractive because the SBA guarantees them over a longer payment period. Since the government is typically on the hook for 80 percent of the loan, the lender only has to stretch to make the 20 percent. In that way a marginal customer might be turned into a sure thing. The interest rates are also attractive, since they are set at 2.75 percent above the prime commercial rate, much better than the credit-card rates women have been paying to finance businesses.

Women have made great strides in getting access to these loans. Less than 8 percent of SBA-guaranteed loans in 1992 were going to women. When Congress renewed the SBA's mandate in 1994, the administration pushed a restructuring that included an SBA commitment to double the number of loans to women and minorities by 1996. In fiscal 1994 alone, the number of loan guarantees to women business owners increased 86 percent, for a total of $1.17 billion, and by mid-1995, 24 percent of the SBA's loan guarantees went to women.

Under the various programs described below—both those for any business and the few specifically targeted to women and minorities—you can find the funding you need.

> **SBA LOAN GUARANTEES**
>
> 1978: less than $3 billion
> 1993: $5.16 billion
> 1995: $8.3 billion
>
> Of that money, the government subsidized $2.74 per $100 loaned. The rest came from lenders and from a borrower guarantee fee of 2 percent of each loan.

> 67,044 businesses were financed by the SBA in 1995, including finance, investment, and bonding programs for a total of more than $8 billion.
>
> Source: Small Business Administration, SBA: A Public/Private Partnership.

THE 7(a) LOAN PROGRAM: BUSINESS LOAN GUARANTEES

The SBA becomes your guarantor or cosigner on your business loan with a commercial bank through its 7(a) basic business loan program ("7(a)" is the title of the section of the SBA act that authorizes the guarantee program).

The SBA guarantees loans of up to $750,000 for many business purposes, such as real estate, expansion, equipment purchases, inventory, and working capital. The SBA guarantees a percentage of the loan—the bank must take the risk on the rest. Usually the SBA guarantees between 70 and 90 percent of the loan amount.

> In 1995, the SBA had reduced its budget by 40 percent and doubled its loan outputs.
>
> Source: The White House, July 1995.

Provided that you are independently owned, do not dominate your field, and can prove that you have been *unable to obtain a bank loan* or other private financing without the SBA's assistance, you can qualify for these loans. You must be turned down by at least one bank, but it does not have to be a different bank from where you ultimately get the loan. So if your bank can't take you as a regular commercial customer, be sure to ask them whether they participate in the SBA loan guarantee programs. (One entrepreneur reported that after going through the application process, she was turned down and never steered to the SBA possibility, even though the bank's telephone message touted the bank's SBA loan program. When she confronted the vice president, she was told, "I didn't see you as an SBA candidate.")

Previously certain "opinion molder" or media companies such as broadcasters, movie theaters, publishers, producers, magazines, newspapers, and distributors of communications were excluded from the SBA's programs because of First Amendment problems (i.e., undue government influence on the press). As of fall 1994 this rule was repealed, so these businesses are now eligible for loans.

7(a) loans have the following characteristics:

Interest rates: Generally, not more than 2.75 percent over prime.
Fees: 2 percent of the guaranteed amount.
Term: Five to seven years for working capital, ten years for fixed assets, twenty-five for real estate acquisitions.
Credit requirements:

- The loan applicant must be of "good character" and demonstrate sufficient management expertise and commitment necessary for success.
- The business must be able to repay its current debts in addition to the new loan payments. Including the new loan, a debt-to-net worth ratio of approximately 3:1 is considered proper.
- The business must have a "reasonable" amount of equity, generally 20 to 30 percent of the amount to start a new business.
- The business must have either strong projections (for a new company) or track record (for an ongoing company).
- Management must have the expertise to conduct the operation of the business.

Application process: The small business submits a loan application to the lender for initial review. The application packet is daunting, to say the least. In fact, it is sufficiently complicated that the lending form contains a notice that the SBA does *not* require that you obtain professional assistance, although it is recommended.

Once you have completed the packet, you submit it to the lender. If the lender finds the application acceptable, it forwards the application and its credit analysis to the nearest SBA office. After SBA approval, the lending institution closes the

SBA 7(a) BUSINESS LOAN PORTFOLIO AS OF 12/31/94

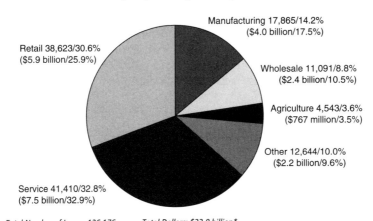

Agencywide by Industry

Manufacturing 17,865/14.2%
($4.0 billion/17.5%)

Retail 38,623/30.6%
($5.9 billion/25.9%)

Wholesale 11,091/8.8%
($2.4 billion/10.5%)

Agriculture 4,543/3.6%
($767 million/3.5%)

Other 12,644/10.0%
($2.2 billion/9.6%)

Service 41,410/32.8%
($7.5 billion/32.9%)

Total Number of Loans: 126,176   Total Dollars: $22.8 billion*

*Of this total, SBA's exposure based on its guaranty is $18.3 billion.

loan and disburses the funds. The borrower then makes loan payments to the lender.

Documentation: The 7(a) applicant must submit:

- financial projections and, for existing businesses, profit and loss statements
- personal financial statements of the owners, including any partner owning 20 percent or more
- an itemized list of how you will use the loan proceeds
- a list of any collateral, detailing its estimated current market value and any liens against the collateral
- a business plan, including background on the principals
- a list of business debt, accounts receivable (and aging of same), and accounts payable
- personal and business tax returns for the past three years
- a copy of the property lease
- any pertinent company contracts or agreements

If these requirements seem overwhelming, then remember, they represent just about exactly what you need for a normal business loan. You'll have to get used to maintaining and providing such information as a businessperson.

Processing time: The SBA itself processes the loans in about ten working days. The hang-ups prior to the processing point center on getting your business plan and the application well prepared. If you go to a SBA preferred lender, that knowledgeable lender will assist you in preparing your packet.

SBA WOMEN'S PREQUALIFICATION LOAN PROGRAM

A Women's Prequalification Pilot Loan Program started in 1994 in sixteen locations. Its purpose, according to the SBA, is to promote the SBA's Business Loan Programs to current and prospective business owners.

This program, which is limited to loans under $250,000, has three steps. First, nonprofit organizations assist prospective women borrowers to develop a viable loan-application package. Second, the package is submitted directly to SBA for a prequalification letter. Third, after approval, the organization can assist the applicant in locating a competitive lender. The criteria stress character, credit, experience, and apparent ability to repay the loan from earnings rather than collateral requirements. By the spring of 1996, the program had issued 690 letters of prequalification, resulting in 501 approved loans totaling $10.5 million dollars.

LowDoc

Because the paperwork for the loans has made applying for them daunting for so many small-business owners, the SBA has created a new "LowDoc" program that simplifies the application process. For loans of $100,000 or less, the application has been reduced to one page. Decisions are made on the application within three days. In the first month

> 63 percent of SBA 7(a) loans were under $100,000 in 1995.
>
> Source: Small Business Administration, SBA: A Public/Private Partnership.

of operation, 26 percent of LowDoc loans went to women-owned businesses. By comparison, women receive about 14 percent of conventional SBA loans. The low maximum loan amount is not a significant impediment to the program. Although the broader program guarantees loans of up to $750,000, the average loan size is only $142,000, so LowDoc is a practical alternative for many applicants.

SBA MICROLOAN PROGRAM

Microloans—minuscule loans of as little as $50—have been a feature of informal associations of entrepreneurs and immigrants both in the United States and in developing countries for many years. As the United States has gotten richer, such programs have given way to more ambitious undertakings, but pockets of such lending programs and other informal support among new immigrants remain strong.

As women have returned from working in international development and seen the importance of such loans in communities throughout the world, this technology has been reimported and put in place within the SBA to help our own communities.

The SBA Microloan program has been based on the fact that two thirds of businesses in this country are started with less than $10,000 and half are launched with under $5,000. Using this information, the SBA set up a program to provide loans of under $50,000 to businesses needing capital. This program has been targeted to assist women, minorities, and low-income entrepreneurs.

To be eligible in many cases, a good reputation in the community will be enough to get the money. The criteria are set by the individual nonprofit agencies to whom the microloans go in bulk quantities to be processed.

Performance on these loans is high: 43 percent go to women and the default rate for the program as a whole is only 3 percent, better than standard commercial lending rates.

> **UNANTICIPATED RESULTS**
>
> The SBA microloan program had so much business in Maine that it inhibited the ability of the local Maine public/private program to make microloans. This "pecuniary externality" or unanticipated consequence illustrates the difficulty of making policies for social change.
>
> Source: Kate Josephs McDonald, loan and investment officer, Coastal Enterprises.

As an initiative to empower the poor and disenfranchised, microlending has an important future, provided that the funds are managed to maintain confidence in the fiduciary responsibility of the program lenders. The potential of these loans for helping women—and men—bootstrap from welfare to small business ownership is tremendous.

THE 504 LOAN PROGRAM: EQUIPMENT FINANCING

Through its 503 and 504 loan programs, the Small Business Administration will guarantee loans used to finance the purchase of tangible assets.

The 504 Loan Program is set up through Certified Development Companies (CDCs), which service small businesses in economically targeted areas. CDC loans provide financing for the acquisition of land, buildings, machinery, equipment, and facility construction or modernization. Normally, the

> 504 assisted projects brought $3.5 billion into play in fiscal year 1994: $2.2 billion from the private sector and $1.3 billion from the 504 Project. The cost to taxpayers was only $6.6 million.
>
> Source: Small Business Administration, SBA: A Public/Private Partnership.

CDC will guide the small business concern through the complex process of obtaining this kind of financing. If you think your business might benefit, contact the nearest SBA office to locate one of the four hundred CDCs nationwide.

The 504 program has recently been streamlined. Since spring 1995, the SBA has serviced CDCs that have a track record with the SBA in three days, making qualification for loans quicker. This new program, called the Accredited Lenders Program (ALP), should help with loan processing under 504.

**GROWTH IN SBA'S SHARE OF BUSINESS LOAN GUARANTEE PROGRAM,
1978–1993**

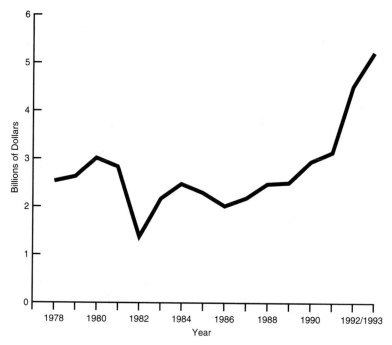

Source: U.S. Small Business Administration, Office of Finance and Investment, 1994, p. 324.

To locate a CDC, contact the Office of Rural Affairs and Economic Development, SBA, 409 Third Street, S.W., Washington, DC 20416 or call 800-8-ASK-SBA.

PROGRAMS THAT ARE NO LONGER FUNDED

Perhaps you've heard of the following programs and wondered if they might be of help. Unfortunately, as we go to press, these programs have lost their funding:

> 502 Loan Program (locally based community development lending)
> SBA Direct Loans (a very small program that included Handicap Assistance Loans as a major feature)

Getting the Government to Invest in You

Capital opportunities with the government are not limited to the SBA's loan programs. Federal and state governments also have programs to spur equity investment in start-up companies. Many of these programs are especially targeted to promote investment in companies with disadvantaged or minority entrepreneurs and those companies focused on developing needed technologies.

Small Business Investment Companies (SBICs)

Thirty-five years ago an entrepreneur looking for capital to launch a small business had no organized market to which to turn. Congress created the Small Business Investment Company (SBIC) Program in 1958. SBICs are licensed by the SBA but are privately organized and privately managed investment firms.

Many analysts credit SBICs with starting the venture capital revolution. SBICs are privately owned, for-profit companies that provide both loans and equity to start-up businesses. SBICs may interest you either as a potential source of financing for your venture or as a business to start.

The appeal of the SBIC to the organizers is the government leverage on the funds provided. The SBA can "leverage" or provide an amount equal to 300 percent of the SBIC's private capital.

SBICs operate like most other venture capital firms, investing equity

> SBICs were original investors in both Intel and Apple Computers.

and debt into new ventures. Generally, SBICs invest in new proprietary technologies or untapped niche markets. If you have that kind of business, you might just find the funding you need.

For the businesswoman looking for capital, the SBIC offers a readily accessible entry point into the world of venture. SBICs can be located through the directory of SBICs, which also lists the main area of focus of each company.*

SSBICs AND MESBICs—301(d)

A special form of SBICs are Specialized Small Business Investment Companies (SSBICs) or Minority Enterprise Small Business Investment Companies (MESBICs). Under Section 301(d) of the Small Business Investment Act, which is still referred to generally by the former name of SSBICs, the SBA will triple the size of a venture fund if that fund targets its investments toward women and minority-owned ventures. In addition, whereas a traditional SBIC must raise $2.5 million before the SBA will provide matching funds, SSBICs need raise only $1.5 million to receive SBA matching funds.

For example, a female-led $1.5 million venture fund dedicated to funding minority-owned businesses could receive matching funds of $4.5 million, allowing a total investment pool of $6 million for the fund. In some circumstances, the amount rises to 400 percent or four times private capital. The maximum amount of SBA matching funds available to an SBIC is $35 million.

*For further information, contact the SBA at 800-827-5722.

STARTING YOUR OWN SBIC

After reading about venture capital, you might feel that the best business for you is as a venture capitalist or VC.

If you are the type of woman who has reached a level of sophistication about money but have not leveraged your own fund-raising abilities beyond your own business, take a look at the SBIC and SSBIC programs. If controlling the funds and helping a number of ventures get off the ground appeals to you, it's not such a long shot.

The steps include raising and committing the necessary capital ($2.5 million for an SBIC and $1.5 million for an SSBIC); preparing a well-structured business plan showing how you will invest the money; and making sure you have qualified management on your staff—management that has at least five years in a responsible business investment position.

It takes four to six months for the SBA to review your application, and the entry price to being considered includes a $5,000 application fee (serious players only need apply). Once your application is approved, you receive an SBIC license and you're ready to receive your matching funds and start investing.

For an overview of the SBIC process, read *Small Business Investment Companies: The SBIC Program.* SBA Investment Division, 409 Third Street, S.W., Washington, DC 20416. To obtain a Licensing Kit, contact the SBA at the above address.

Small Business Innovative Research Grants

Small Business Innovative Research grants (SBIRs) provide funding for start-up companies that are focused on developing specific technologies requested by the government. For example, the National Institute of Health lists the health-care technologies most sought by the government and solicits business proposals by entrepreneurs capable of developing those technologies.

The Small Business Innovative Research program was created in 1982 to attract new technologically oriented companies to needed science and engineering research. The SBIR funding comes in stages, and at each stage the completion of the technical developments must be complete before the additional funds are committed.

The typical Phase I application includes the following:

- identification and significance of the project or opportunity
- Phase I technical objectives
- Phase I work plan
- related work of the applicant to the technology

- relationship with future research and development
- potential applications for later phases
- key personnel
- facilities and equipment
- consultants
- prior, current, or pending support
- cost proposal detailing expected expenses

In essence, the SBIR application is a business plan, and the grants can be start-up funding for a new venture even though the terms are primarily based on a specific research and development project.

All federal agencies with outside research and development budgets exceeding $100 million annually participate in the SBIR program, including: Agriculture, Commerce, Defense, Education, Energy, HHS, Transportation, the EPA, and NASA. Each agency sets aside a small portion of its research budget for the program. For more information, contact the relevant agency directly.

State Programs

Similar to the federal SBIC and SBIR programs, many states have venture capital pools created to fund local companies. These state programs work in a manner similar to regionally focused, traditional venture capital firms. Typically, business plans are accepted for review only from companies operating within the state because the goal of the program is primarily to increase employment opportunities and commercial tax revenue for the state. Profits from the state venture fund are normally reinvested by the fund.

For more information about state venture pools, contact your state's department of commerce.

Contracting for Work with the Government

"Procurement," or doing business with the government as your customer, is a major potential source of revenue for your company. Many construction, high-tech, and manufacturing companies focus almost exclusively on servicing the government. In fact, cutbacks in defense spending had such a significant impact on some corporations that they caused a severe recession in certain regional economies such as southern California.

The government spends approximately $200 billion a year on the procurement of goods and services. Because of the size of the stakes involved, procurement has been a major focus for female, minority, and small-business activists. Of the $200 billion contracted by the

> ### WOMEN-LED BUSINESSES AND FEDERAL PROCUREMENT
>
> 34 percent of small businesses are owned by women, but only 1.1 percent of prime contracts over $25,000 were awarded to women-owned businesses.
>
> *Source: Federal Procurement Data System, 1992 Fiscal Year Report.*

government, a total of 18 percent was awarded directly to small businesses, not including indirect subcontracting.

Doing business with the government, especially the federal government, can range from selling multibillion-dollar defense projects to providing janitorial services to contracting for the construction of federal office buildings, with a range of opportunities in between.

The Procurement Process

Contracting for work with the federal government can be accomplished in one of two ways. Procurement contracts are awarded directly by the various federal agencies and departments through what are known as *prime contracts*. The second method involves indirect purchases by *subcontract* with the SBA or another federal business contractor.

Both military and civilian purchasing occurs throughout the country to spread business around to different geographic localities and to save on transportation costs that would be involved if the government were to purchase in one or two locations only. This regional or local buying means that you don't have to travel to Washington, D.C., to do business with the government.

In theory, a women-led business would follow the standard procedures, which involve either a *sealed bidding* or *negotiation* process.

With sealed bidding, a purchasing office sends bid invitations to firms that are listed on their solicitation mailing list (for the most part, if you want to be in the process, your company must be on the list). In addition, often the purchasing office will want to obtain offers from additional firms not on the list. You can find these notices in the *Commerce Business Daily* (*CBD*), a daily publication that lists all major federal government solicitations, contract awards, subcontracting leads, surplus-property sales, and foreign business opportunities expected to cost more than $100,000. These notices, or "invitations for bids" (IFBs), include the specifications for the proposed purchase and other information necessary to complete a bid.

A *CBD* subscription currently costs $208 a year via second-class mail and $261 via first-class mail. To subscribe, contact the Government Printing Office, Washington, DC 20402. The *CBD* can also be found at most public libraries.

On a designated day, the sealed bids will be opened in public. The low bidder will get the contract, assuming that it meets specifications.

By contrast, when buying by negotiation, procedures vary. Negotiated buying often involves technologies that are not widely supplied by small businesses, such as military hardware. Through Requests for Proposal (RFPs) or Requests for Quotation (RFQs), the government attempts to make the negotiated process more competitive.

Often the bidding and negotiation process itself is so costly and time-consuming that small businesses find it difficult to participate, even when more standard items that they might reasonably supply are required.

At the opposite extreme of formality and size, the noncompetitive bidding process involves "simplified acquisition threshold" contracts which are awarded for less than $100,000—small potatoes to the government, but a large opportunity for specialized firms. Research firms and others providing highly specialized work find this process particularly rewarding. Unlike the RFP process, the noncompetitive bidding contracts aren't publicly listed. You have to identify an area of information or activity that you think an agency of government needs and then figure out who has the budget authority and budget to buy that product or service. In reality, this process involves both what and who you know (although it's by no means a pork barrel). Many vital research projects are carried out under this process where, for one reason or another, the government requires information that cannot be produced in-house.

Small businesses in general aren't as equipped as large corporations to jump through the legal and bureaucratic hoops necessary to do business with the government. Both the formal and informal processes have been heavily criticized in recent years, leading to the passage in late 1994 of the Federal Acquisition Streamlining Act (FASA), designed to include small businesses in the procurement process.

Aside from the costs of bidding, small businesses were discouraged by the extensive paperwork and long payment delays involved in federal procurement. One goal of the FASA legislation was to speed up the delivery of contract dollars to federal suppliers so that small businesses would be able to compete with larger, more heavily capitalized firms.

Among other innovations, the act put in place a FACNET electronic

---

PURCHASING POWER

Even a small change in the percentage of federal contracts awarded to women would have a huge impact—$200 billion is spent in annual government procurement.

Source: Small Business Administration.

DEPARTMENT OF DEFENSE (DOD) SHARE OF FEDERAL CONTRACTS

Women-owned businesses tend to stay out of the defense industry, yet that is where most of the federal procurement dollars have gone.

DOD, 1992	67.7%
DOD, 1990	74.9%
DOD, 1985*	80.1%

*All-time high.

Source: "The State of Small Business," 1994.

bidding and purchasing process, even for firms in rural areas. The act also requires the purchase of "commercial items" rather than special (and costly) custom products. This requirement allows small firms an opportunity to seek to meet federal needs with off-the-shelf goods and services rather than complex defense projects, something that small business is better equipped to do. All contracts from $2,500 to $100,000 are set aside for small businesses unless the contracting officer cannot find offers from two or more capable small firms.

> "Some experts believe that small firms, with their inherent flexibility, fit into the niches of marginal spending more effectively than their larger counterparts, and so will perform better than large firms during a downswing in military procurement. With continued military downsizing, there are likely to be new opportunities to test this notion."
>
> —"The State of Small Business: A Report of the President" (Washington, DC: U.S. Government Printing Office, 1994), p. 357

This change could be *critical* for women-led and minority-led businesses, considering the current anti–affirmative action political climate. Since women- and minority-led businesses account for almost 40 percent of all small businesses, this provision of the 1994 act will give both groups something to fall back on if other programs, such as Title 8(a), are abolished or severely curtailed.

For an overview of the federal procurement process, see *Procurement Assistance: A Practical Guide for Businesses Seeking Federal Contracts*, available from the SBA Office of Procurement Assistance, 800-8-ASK-SBA.

Women-Owned Small Business Prime Contracts

Prime contracts represent the cream of the government crop. Prime contracts are defined as contracts made directly with the government, not through a government or other subcontractor.

Of the $39.9 billion in prime contracts awarded to small business in 1992, women-owned small businesses received $2.9 billion. ("The State of Small Business: A Report of the President," 1994, pp. 352, 401.) This figure amounted to a 1.4 percent share of government business in the same year for women-led concerns.

PROCUREMENT GOAL SETTING

In 1988, Congress set a 20 percent procurement goal for small businesses.

By 1992, the small business share of federal procurement dollars stood at 30.8 percent, including subcontracting.

In 1994, the Federal Acquisition Streamlining Act (FASA) set a goal of 5 percent for women-owned businesses.

Source: NWBC Compendium of National Statistics on Women-Owned Business in the U.S., 1994, p. 5-1, and "The State of Small Business: A Report of the President," p. 352.

The government estimates that about 50,000 firms compete effectively for the lion's share of contracts, suggesting that the government officials, like most of us, do business by habit. Returning repeatedly to the same businesses provides comfort and predictability for the contracting officers—and exclusion by habit for women-led firms. To break these old habits, women-owned businesses must aggressively market to the government.

If you have the kind of business that might be able to sell successfully to the government, go after prime contracts. The women's business advocates within the agencies, discussed below, can help point your way.

DISTRIBUTION OF PRIME CONTRACT ACTIONS OVER $25,000 BY MAJOR PRODUCT OR SERVICE CATEGORY FOR SELECTED YEARS

1992 Total	*All Small Businesses*	*Women-Owned Businesses*
Research and development	16.4%	8.5%
Construction	7.1%	48.1%
Services	36.8%	17.0%
Supplies and equipment	39.7%	12.1%

Source: SBA, "The State of Small Business: A Report of the President" (Washington, DC: U.S. Government Printing Office, 1994).

THE OVERALL BARRIER TO GOVERNMENT CONTRACTING FOR WOMEN: BUSINESS FIT

Government contracting has been done primarily in industries where women-owned businesses are scarce, such as the defense industry. Irrespective of discrimination, women's businesses haven't been a good fit. Over 70 percent of women's businesses are in the service sector with fewer than five employees, while the majority of federal contracting falls to larger-scale enterprises producing defense materials. To illustrate the size of the gap, think about these figures: 2 percent of the number of federal contracts accounts for 89 percent of all federal procurement dollars. The remaining 11 percent of expenditures, or $22 billion (out of $200 billion in procurement dollars), are spread out among *all* the remaining federal contractors, including women-led businesses.

PROCUREMENT FOR WOMEN: DISTRIBUTION TO WOMEN-OWNED BUSINESSES (WOBs)

	Of All WOBs	*Procurement to Small Businesses*	*Procurement to WOBs*
Construction	N/A	43.17%	3.29%
Mining	N/A	28.53%	3.67%
Total construction and mining	6.97%	71.70%	6.96%
Manufacturing	6.29%	9.79%	0.61%
Transportation	2.98%	16.04%	3.12%
Wholesale trade	7.02%	40.25%	3.70%
Retail trade	26.95%	71.64%	16.69%
Finance/insurance/ real estate	4.93%	36.76%	1.33%
Services	44.85%	16.57%	1.66%

Sources: Federal Reserve Bulletin, July 1995 (1993 data for share of all women-owned businesses), and the Small Business Administration, Office of Government Contracting, unpublished data, 1994.

COMPARABLE WORTH

Briefly stated, the principle of comparable worth suggests women are paid lower wages compared to men because the type of jobs women dominate tend to be paid less than those dominated by men.

In some ways the problem is parallel to the comparable worth issue. The fact that men dominate the industries with which the government does business may be a product of that business as much as it is a product of the choices women make. Much of our economy is shaped by government purchasing power—from the aerospace industry to steel manufacturing. One SBA study showed that when the federal government purchased within a particular business sector, the sector was strengthened. Because of the potential size of the contracts involved, when women-led businesses get a larger share of the federal purchasing pie, we can expect to see more major women-led corporations.

For an overview of selling to the government prepared especially for women-led businesses, ask the SBA for *Women Business Owners: Selling to the Federal Government*. Unfortunately, it is not a substitute for information from each individual department.

PROCUREMENT—THE FIVE PERCENT SOLUTION

Through the efforts of the women's business lobby, in 1994 Congress enacted regulations requiring all federal agencies to set a 5 percent procurement goal with women-owned businesses. In the previous decade, a voluntary program of contracting to women-owned businesses had placed less than 1 percent of all federal contracts in women's hands. At the end of 1994, women had received 2.8 percent of all contracts for a total of $4.9 billion dollars.

Assistance to Minorities and Others— 8(a): Federal Contracting

In addition to general efforts to open procurement on a department-by-department basis, a specialized form of procurement is available for minority and other disadvantaged businesses through Section 8(a). Under the Section 8(a) program, the government acts as a general contractor, awarding subcontracts to businesses that meet the 8(a) criteria.

To participate in the 8(a) program, a business must be at least 51 percent unconditionally owned by either:

- an individual(s) who is a socially and economically disadvantaged citizen of the United States; or
- an economically disadvantaged member of an Indian tribe, including a native Alaskan corporation or an economically disadvantaged native Hawaiian organization.

PROCUREMENT FOR WOMEN

Despite the 5 percent target, only 2 percent of all prime federal procurement contracts were awarded to women in 1994. The departments offering the largest share of their procurement contracts to women were not the departments awarding the most procurement dollars to women.

AGENCIES AWARDING THE MOST CONTRACT DOLLARS TO WOMEN

Defense	$1.857 billion
Energy	$418.2 million
GSA	$163.2 million
Transportation	$55.1 million
HHS	$149.6 million

AGENCIES AWARDING THE LARGEST SHARE OF THEIR CONTRACT DOLLARS TO WOMEN

HUD	6.9%
Treasury	5.4%
Interior	4.7%
Commerce	4.5%
State	4.2%

Source: National Women's Business Council and SBA.

Further tests of economic and social disadvantage include:

- A presumption of social disadvantage is extended to citizens whose background is African American, Native American, Puerto Rican, Spanish-speaking, Eskimo, Aleut, or Asian. Those not a member of these groups must qualify by establishing a pattern of social disadvantage on the basis of clear and convincing evidence.
- Economic disadvantage can be established if personal net worth does not exceed $250,000, exclusive of equity in a primary residence or investment in the business.

Although there are no specific gender-related set-asides, it is possible for women business owners to gain access to the program if they meet the above criteria.

Once firms are admitted to the program, they may participate for nine years. During that time they are assisted in their individual business development programs through a combination of management and technical assistance, in addition to federal contracting opportunities.

To find out more about the program, contact the Contracting Officers, SBA Office of Minority Enterprise Development at the SBA. Phone: 800-532-1169 or 202-366-1938; fax 202-366-7538.

During the last few years, Section 8(a) has been brought under fire. Complaints have arisen about abuse of the definition of "economically disadvantaged," as well as perceived inefficiencies of the program. In the *Adarand Constructors, Inc.* vs. *Peña* ruling, the Supreme Court ordered the federal government to meet more rigorous standards for affirmative action, not to dismantle it. "Set-asides," or programs that give preference to women and minorities, must be targeted to particular regions and business areas where problems of discrimination or exclusion are provable and affirmative action is clearly required. In response, a July 1995 story in the *Wall Street Journal* noted "The White House also wants to end the excessive use of minority or women-owned companies in particular regions or industries" (7/19/95, p. 10).

In addition, stories and allegations have been circulated about "underqualified" businesses winning contracts solely because of their 8(a) status. The *Government Executive* reported in June 1995 that because the Defense Department was required to award 5 percent of the value of its contracts to "social and economically disadvantaged" people in small business, an anomalous result was achieved: "Because much of the DOD's procurement spending goes for high-tech research and weapons production, meeting this quota hasn't been easy. As a result, a disproportionate amount of relatively low-tech contracting goes to minority-operated firms in such fields as construction."

> "Before it was very difficult to get in the door. They were always asking for past experience. Now [with Title 8(a)] I get to prove myself."
>
> —Jaimie Beaman, architect, quoted in Bureau of National Affairs, Daily Labor Report, 13 June 1995

Despite its adversaries, Section 8(a) has been essential in getting minority female entrepreneurs funding and experience. Because of discrimination and habit in selecting contractors, minority- and women-led businesses did not have a fair chance of competing, establishing themselves in new industries, and gaining experience. Given the potential impact the vast federal procurement pool can have on small businesses, the focus of Section 8(a) has enabled many minority female entrepreneurs to successfully grow their businesses and enter nontraditional industries.

Regardless of the success of the program, now that the program has had an impact—and minority- and women-owned businesses are viewed as a viable source of contracting and competition—the political tide has turned against affirmative action. The 1995 *Adarand* decision brought the fate of such programs into question.

The Clinton administration, in response to the Supreme Court ruling and Congressional affirmative action critics, put in place four new standards. These include:

- no quotas in theory or practice
- no illegal discrimination, including reverse discrimination
- no preference for people who are not qualified for a job or opportunity
- no permanent programs

Section 8(a) is a government program meant to serve the needs of all citizens. If as a woman business owner, you think these programs should be retained, let your member of Congress and your U.S. Senators know your views.

When Section 8(a) began in 1969, minority-owned firms had only $11 million in federal contracts. Since then, the program has awarded $18 billion in contracts to such companies and is now responsible for almost half of the federal contract dollars awarded to minority firms.*

*Editor's note: By the spring of 1996, nearly $50 billion in federal contracting dollars had been channeled into 8(a) firms.

Source: Arlene Zarembka, "Longing for the Good Ol' Boy's Network," St. Louis Post-Dispatch, 16 April 1995.

"The *Adarand* decision did not dismantle affirmative action and did not dismantle set-asides. In fact, while setting stricter standards to mandate reform of affirmative action, it actually reaffirmed the need for affirmative action and reaffirmed the continuing existence of systematic discrimination in the United States."

—President Bill Clinton, 1995

Other Women-Friendly Federal Agencies

Aside from the Small Business Administration, many agencies of the federal government offer special programs of interest to women business owners. If your business falls in a specialized, technical, or obscure area, look for the federal agency that oversees that

Most federal departments and agencies now have an Office of Small and Disadvantaged Business Utilization (OSDBU) which serves women- and minority-owned businesses. Start there if you don't know where to start within the government.

sector. The likelihood is that programs will exist that can provide you either with assistance and information or with contract opportunities. Many programs are offered to support small businesses. The following are key agency programs that may offer opportunities for women business owners because of what they buy or their track record in dealing with women. Others offer tremendous opportunities because of the size of their purchasing budget, so they cannot be overlooked.

Most agencies offer a publication that tells how to market to that particular agency with a list of contacts, purchasing agents, and a copy of "Forecast Opportunities" for small businesses for the fiscal year. Contact the agencies directly.

THE DEPARTMENT OF AGRICULTURE

The department has a pamphlet called *Selling to the USDA*. In addition, the department is trying to increase the number of women-owned businesses on its mailing lists.

The USDA illustrates specifics of how women-led businesses are missing in certain markets. Agricultural women-owned businesses are hard to find; the spokesperson at the USDA Small Business office said that women-owned construction companies were easier to locate.*

THE DEPARTMENT OF COMMERCE

The Department of Commerce has the overall responsibility for facilitating business in the United States. Through this department, many programs are available for all businesses, while the SBA concentrates exclusively on businesses involving 500 or fewer employees. The department is a prime source of information through The Census Bureau and the Bureau of Economic Analysis. These two bureaus generate the data and analyses that depict the structure and status of the entire U.S. economy and its interactions with the rest of the world; the characteristics and trends of American business; the size, location, and characteristics of the American population; and the principal features and trends of American society. For market analysis, the Commerce Department and its publications are a must.

The Patent and Trademark Office is contained within Commerce, for those with businesses to protect, as well as the International Trade Administration (ITA) to facilitate export of U.S. products.

The Commerce Minority Business Development Agency (MBDA) coordinates federal efforts to develop and strengthen new and existing minority businesses. If you are a minority business owner, contact the MBDA for information, advice, and networking. Many regional Minority Business Development Centers, Native American Business Development Centers, regional Minority Enterprise Growth Assistance Centers, Business Resource Centers and Minority Business Opportunity Committees form a network of business assistance available to minority-owned businesses. For nonminority women business owners, the department does not offer a distinct agency but has encouraged contracting offices to take action to assist women-owned business in securing a fair proportion of contracts. The department also has special efforts underway to identify women in high-tech businesses and include them in the Small Business Innovative Research (SBIR) program.

From a procurement point of view, the Commerce Department offers annual procurement trade fairs as well as publications.

---

*You can contact the USDA at 202-720-7117.

Depending on the final outcome of federal budget negotiations in coming years, the Commerce Department may be restructured.

For more information, contact the Minority Business Development Agency, *Business Development Center Directory*, Department of Commerce, Washington, DC 20230. Phone 202-482-4671.

THE DEPARTMENT OF DEFENSE

The Defense Department is the largest source of federal procurement dollars. Unfortunately for women, the department spends most of its money in one industry where women are not—defense. Selling to the military might seem to be an impossible proposition if you look at the list of products and services bought by major military purchasing offices, which include:

- guns
- chemical weapons
- launchers
- degassing and mine-sweeping equipment
- camouflage and deception equipment

But look further. There are some purchasing requirements by the Defense Department that many existing women-owned businesses can easily provide, because the list also includes:

- furniture
- household and commercial furnishings and appliances
- office machines
- books, maps, and other publications
- musical instruments, phonographs, and home radios
- toiletries

While most women-owned businesses don't approach the scale necessary to deliver artillery, many could supply some of the more ordinary items that support military administration and personnel.

For more information, obtain the publication *Selling to the Military: Army, Navy, Air Force, Defense Logistics Agency, and Other Defense Agencies* from the U.S. Government Printing Office, Superintendent of Documents, Mail Stop: SSOP, Washington, DC 20402-9328.

THE DEPARTMENT OF HEALTH AND HUMAN SERVICES

The Department of Health and Human Services oversees the federal delivery of health services and welfare. Among its programs aimed at improving women business owners' access to procurement, the department cosponsors women-owned business expos with the SBA, looks for joint venture arrangements with other firms, and seeks to include women in SBIRs, most notably in the National Action Plan on Breast Cancer and other programs that foster innovations and technology. (In addition, the department now requires that grants funded by the National Institutes of Health must report the number of women being studied and the gender component of the study— good news for the health of women business owners.) The Department's "JOLI" program also gives grants to groups that work with low income/welfare women to train them for jobs or their own enterprises.

For more information on HHS, contact the Department of Health and Human Services, Office of Small and Disadvantaged Business Utilization, Washington, DC 20201. Phone 202-690-7300.

THE DEPARTMENT OF TRANSPORTATION (DOT)

The DOT serves as the focal point in the federal government for the coordinated national transportation policy and implementation. The department consists of seven administrations, each representing the various transportation modes. The agencies include: The U.S. Coast Guard, Federal Aviation Administration (FAA), Federal Highway Administration, Federal Railroad Administration, National Highway Traffic Safety Administration, Federal Transit Administration, Saint Lawrence Seaway Development Corporation, and Maritime Administration and Research and Special Programs Administration.

As with the Department of Defense, although much of the purchasing consists of high-tech equipment, opportunities to sell to the department do exist for women. In addition to general contracting, the department purchases everything from computer software to storage tanks.

Obtain the Department of Transportation, *Marketing Information Package*, Office of Small and Disadvantaged Business Utilization, 400 7th Street, SW, Washington, DC 20590. Phone 202-366-1930 or 800-532-1169; fax 202-366-7538. This user-friendly, comprehensive report will tell you all you need to know to market to the DOT and its agencies.

Pushing Procurement for Women

The importance of increasing procurement to women has taken a front seat in the efforts of women-owned business advocates. Even a slight change in the current proportion of contracts awarded to women will have a significant impact on women-owned businesses, given the $200 billion size of the federal procurement pool.

WOMEN'S PROCUREMENT PILOT PROGRAM WOMEN'S ADVOCATES

Department of Agriculture, OSDBU, Washington, DC 20250. Phone 202-720-7117.

Department of Defense, OSDBU, 361 Defense Pentagon, Washington, DC 20301-3061. Phone 703-697-9383.

Department of Energy, Office of Impact, 1000 Independence Ave., Washington, DC 20585. Phone 202-586-8383.

Department of Health and Human Services, OSDBU, Washington, DC 20201. Phone 202-690-6670.

Department of Housing and Urban Development, Washington, DC 20585. Phone 202-708-1428.

Department of Justice, OSDBU, ARB Room 3235, Washington, DC 20530. Phone 202-616-0521.

Department of Labor, Office of Small Business and Minority Affairs, 200 Constitution Avenue, NW, Washington, DC 20210. Phone 202-219-9148.

Department of Transportation, OSDBU, Washington, DC 20590. Phone 202-366-1930.

Environmental Protection Agency, OSDBU, Washington, DC 20460. Phone 703-305-7777

General Services Administration, 18th and F Streets, Washington, DC 20405. Phone 202-501-4466.

National Aeronautics and Space Administration Headquarters, Washington, DC 20546-0001. Phone 202-358-2088.

To carry out the ambitious 5 percent program, two legislatively mandated groups are working within the federal bureaucracy. One, the Inter-Agency Committee on Women's Business Enterprise, consists of top appointees of the president, such as cabinet secretaries and their support staff. Their mission is to set policies and procedures that support opportunities for women-led business within the federal agencies; we'll discuss them below.

On the implementation side, all agencies operate an Office of Disadvantaged and Small Businesses Utilization (ODSBU). These offices help small businesses, in general, within the procurement process. An expansion of that program has occurred with the women-owned business procurement pilot program, which has advocates in several agencies whose job it is to help women owners with the information they need to do business with their agency.

WOMEN-OWNED BUSINESS PROCUREMENT PILOT PROGRAM

To overcome the barriers to procurement for women, the SBA has developed a pilot program to increase the federal procurement dollars awarded to businesses owned and operated by women. Key federal agencies participate in the program to develop a systematic approach to expand the number of women-owned firms receiving federal contract awards.

The plan involves connecting women-owned business advocates with the SBA and women business owners to provide outreach, training, and marketing assistance. Within the government, SBA representatives will meet monthly to coordinate.

The program focuses on educating women to the procurement process as well as increasing their access to federal procurement. The program will also strive to register women in the SBA's Procurement Automated Source System (PASS), a database of contractors seeking federal procurement awards. The agencies involved in the program will be encouraged to use PASS to identify women-owned businesses to meet their contracting needs.

The Federal Procurement Report offers an overview of the federal procurement process, with valuable information about government buying patterns. To do business with a specific agency, however, you need to look at that agency's needs and see if your business matches their requirements.

Affecting Government Policy

In our democracy, the government is supposed to respond to the demands of the people. As a majority of the voting population, women have a strong voice, as do small businesses, which comprise 95 percent of all businesses.

The Small Business Administration is the prime small business advocate within the federal government and offers the most immediate practical assistance aimed at women. Over the past few years, the agency has been fine-tuning its programs to be more responsive to women's particular needs. The SBA has an Office of Women's Business Ownership and works in conjunction with the National Women's Business Council (NWBC) to promote policies and programs fostering women business owners. In addition, several federal agencies and departments are actively advocating changes to involve and provide opportunities for women within the government. Most directly, your congresspeople have been elected to serve the needs of their constituents and remain an important channel for directing your concerns as a female entrepreneur and a voter.

The National Women's Business Council

Created in 1988 by an act of Congress and reorganized in 1994, the National Women's Business Council (NWBC) is "an independent source of advice and policy recommendations" to the Inter-Agency Committee, the SBA, Congress, and the president.

The NWBC's five private representatives (appointed from various women's business organizations) work with the executive director and her staff as national clearinghouse for information about women-led businesses. The council provides formal policy input and constantly strives to educate politicians and bureaucrats about the issues facing women in business. The council has been particularly active in helping set the agenda for women in business at the federal level, at the SBA, and through the legislature, including the legislatively mandated 5 percent federal procurement goal for women-owned businesses.

The Office of Women's Business Ownership

The Office of Women's Business Ownership (OWBO) is the primary program office within the SBA for women and business owners. The OWBO has served as both an advocate for women and an access point to the government for women business owners. During the 1970s and early 1980s, OWBO gathered statistics on women's business ownership which have become an invaluable baseline for us today. Although the office fell on hard budgetary times from the mid-1980s until the change of administration in 1992, it is now alive and active on behalf of women. OWBO's programs include technical, financial and management information, and information on selling to the federal government.

For more information on OWBO, contact the Deputy Director of the SBA and Director, Office of Women's Business Ownership, 409 Third Street, S.W., Washington, DC 20416. Phone 202-205-6673.

The SBA Advisory Committee

THE INTER-AGENCY TASK FORCE ON WOMEN IN BUSINESS

The Inter-Agency Committee on Women's Business Enterprise, although congressionally mandated in 1994, was first created by executive order in 1977 by President Jimmy Carter. The task force produced a report on women's business progress called *The Bottom Line: Unequal Enterprise in America* in 1978.

The report found a "paucity" of data. Only one government report had been done on women in business in U.S. history, that in 1972. That report showed a picture that the task force labeled "askew." There was absolutely no information on the entrepreneur herself. A supplementary survey conducted

WOMEN IN BUSINESS, 1972

- Women-owned businesses were 4.6 percent of all U.S. large and small firms.
- Receipts totaled $8.1 billion, only 0.3 percent of all U.S. business receipts.
- Women-owned businesses were clustered in labor-intensive industries that required low capitalization and tended to show a lower return on investment.
- 98 percent of women-owned firms were sole proprietorships.
- Only 13 percent of the firms had paid employees.

Source: Department of Commerce, The Bottom Line: Unequal Enterprise in America. *Report of the President's Inter-Agency Task Force on Women Business Owners, Department of Commerce (Washington, DC: Government Printing Office, June 1978), p. 6.*

through the task force's auspices revealed that most women business owners surveyed had little education for their tasks, mostly drawing their entrepreneurial skills from work experience. "The Task Force found that the problem of education in entrepreneurship lay in inadequate preparation for business and in attitudes that limited career options and aspirations." In addition to problems in the formal educational arena, the task force found that "there are also limited opportunities in either the public or private sectors for prospective entrepreneurs to get needed management training."

The task force also noted that "acceptance of women's capabilities by the financial community is slow in coming and that women are still subject to subtle discrimination. Although legislation such as the Equal Credit Opportunity Act (ECOA) of 1974 has been of significant importance," commercial credit was hard to obtain. The report continued: "Nor has the financial community yet recognized the market potential of women as business owners."

THE INTER-AGENCY COMMITTEE ON WOMEN'S BUSINESS ENTERPRISE, 1996

- Chair: National Economic Council, Assistant to President
- Commerce
- Defense
- Executive Office of the President, Office of Women's Outreach and Initiatives
- Federal Reserve Governor
- Government Services Administration
- Health and Human Services
- Labor, Women's Bureau
- SBA, Office of Women's Business Ownership
- Transportation
- Treasury

Writing less than two decades ago, the task force saw reason for hope, but it could never have predicted the burgeoning marketplace we see now. While many of the problems are the same, the scope and magnitude of the arena has changed enormously in less than twenty years.

The Department of Labor Women's Bureau

The Women's Bureau at the Department of Labor is the longest-running federal office devoted exclusively to women. The office was inaugurated under the leadership of Labor Secretary Frances Perkins, the first woman ever to hold cabinet rank, from 1933 to 1945.

The Department of Labor, Office of Small Business and Minority Affairs, has satellite offices around the country which can be reached by calling 202-219-6593.

A Primer on Dealing with the Federal Government

Now that we've looked at the formal structure of the programs within the federal government, it's time to take a step back and remind ourselves of how our federal tripartite system works. From high school civics, you remember the three key branches:

- the executive
- the legislative
- the judiciary

While the judiciary, in the form of the Supreme Court, hasn't much to do with your day-to-day search for capital (but keep an eye on those affirmative action decisions—they can hamper or help you a great deal), the legislature mustn't be overlooked when you seek federal loans or procurement opportunities.

Your member of Congress and senators can and should assist you if you get stuck dealing with any federal agency. All federal agencies are overworked, tabloid reports to the contrary. To get the attention of an official in a timely fashion or to overcome stumbling blocks placed in your way by rules that should be adjusted for your situation, your legislator can help you. A letter or call "from the Hill" (Congress) works wonders in the executive branch (federal agencies such as the SBA and HUD).

Each congressional office is set up with assistants who specialize in different specific areas of government. You need to write your representative or senator, then follow up by phone, fax, or an in-person visit with the "legislative assistant" who is responsible for your area of concern. Despite the low-level title, these folks have a lot of power. They know the agencies and can help you through many bureaucratic hurdles. If all else fails, contact your congressperson's "administrative assistant," the equivalent of an executive assistant, for your representative or senator.

A word of caution: It is proper to help get the policy or procedure to work the way it should or to get appropriate adjustments. It is improper to use your contact to influence a decision in a way contrary to that policy or procedure. Obviously, the line between the two is sometimes thin, but err on the side of caution to avoid any impropriety.

Our system of checks and balances makes it the job of the legislative branch to oversee the executive branch (including the agencies). By helping you, your senators and representatives are accomplishing part of that task by keeping the operation of government running smoothly for the end-user, you, the citizen. Don't be shy about asking for help if you need it.

Change in the women's business arena occurs at lightning speed now. To keep pace with the explosion of this business sector, to check on new developments, and generally to keep informed, get on key mailing lists. Also check in your local area for women in business seminars and conferences. These too can keep you in tune with the times. Try to keep your elected officials informed about women's business issues as well.

Resources and References

The National Women's Business Council is an excellent resource for interacting with the federal government, as well as the national women's networking organizations. The NWBC is also at the forefront of educating federal policy makers by providing current information on women in business. Several NWBC reports have been used in writing this book, including: *1994 Annual Report to the President of the United States and the Congress of the United States* (Washington, DC: NWBC, 1995); *1993 Annual Report to the President and Congress* (Washington, DC: NWBC, 1994); *Access to Equity Capital: Expert Policy Workshop, Federal Reserve Bank of Chicago* (Washington, DC: NWBC, 1994); and most importantly, *A Compendium of National Statistics on Women-Owned Businesses in the U.S.* (Washington, DC: NWBC, 1994). The NWBC can be reached at National Women's Business Council, 409 Third Street, S.W., Washington, DC 20416; phone 202-205-3850.

Accessing the Small Business Administration: With its aggressive entry into on-line service, the SBA has become more accessible. The SBA can be reached by mail at U.S. Small Business Administration, 409 Third Street, S.W., Washington, DC 20416; by phone at 800-8-ASK-SBA; or on-line at http://wwwsbaonline.sba.gov. But note: Today the SBA has finally developed a market-driven, customer-service attitude, but with budget pressures constantly looming, your success in working with the SBA may vary. Like all bureaucracies, the SBA can be frustrating. Phones are busy and people don't always know everything you need to know. Persistence does pay in dealing with any agency, especially if you believe they have something to offer you.

Accessing Congress: Use your member and their staff, as noted. Each area of government also has a congressional committee and senate committee that oversees it. The *Congressional Staff Directory* has Hill and committee staff listed by name and phone number. You can write to your representative via U.S. Congress, Washington, DC 20515. Your senators can be reached via U.S. Senate, Washington, DC 20510. The congressional switchboard number is 202-224-3121.

Accessing the executive branch: Buy or get in the library Congressional Quarterly's *Who's Who in the Federal Executive Branch*, published annually, for a thumbnail overview of the federal executive, with names and phone numbers. Congressional Quarterly, Inc., 1414 22nd Street N.W., Washington, DC 20037. Phone 800-638-1710; fax 202-887-6706. Or, if your research into the far reaches of government requires more precise data, check out the larger *Congressional Staff Directory*. Order from Staff Directories, Ltd., Mount Vernon, VA 22121-0062. Phone 703-739-0900; fax 703-739-0234.

For more information about procurement in general, contact The Office of Government Contracting and Minority Enterprise Development, SBA, Washington, DC 20416. Phone 202-205-6459.

The State of Small Business: A Report of the President, Transmitted to the Congress (Washington: Government Printing Office) is an annual report providing a detailed overview of small business and the American economy.

Small Business Administration, *The White House Conference on Small Business: Issue Handbook*, 2d ed. (Washington, DC: SBA, 1995) detailed the issues most pressing to small business leaders in 1995.

U.S. Chamber of Commerce/IBM, *The Small Business Resource Guide: Government and Private-Sector Assistance for Small and Growing Companies* (Washington, DC: Braddock Communications, 1994) provides a listing of contact numbers for resources available to small businesses.

If you are planning to work with the SBA, consider Gustav Berle's *SBA Hotline: Answer Book* (New York: John Wiley & Sons, 1992) and Patrick D. O'Hara's *SBA Loans: A Step-by-Step Guide*, 2d ed. (New York: John Wiley & Sons, 1994).

Office of Women's Business Ownership, *Women Business Owners: Selling to the Federal Government*. (Washington, DC: U.S. Small Business Administration, 1990) provides some guidance on procurement.

CHAPTER 5

Specialized Sources of Management Development, Capital, and Information

Capital hangs out in the most unlikely places, especially when you count intellectual and human capital—both essentials in starting businesses that last. Private organizations created to support women business owners, state and local governments, institutions, pension funds, foundations, and business development centers can all be important sources for your business.

One key purpose of this chapter is to point you toward some programs that you may not have considered, such as state-sponsored training programs and other training opportunities. A second purpose is to provide clues to specialized sources of capital. We also look at several management and informational programs that will lead women to capital opportunities.

If you need capital, don't overlook these organizations. Even though you might not be in the mood for informational programming, with seminars and training specifically targeted to women, you'll get structure, guidance, and moral support from leaders and colleagues in a nonstressful learning environment. Some of the organizations offer crossover programs in which cash grants are available to those entrepreneurs participating in their training programs. Other organizations work specifically to achieve social change, some of it directed at women and girls, others directed at entrepreneurship. These organizations offer direct assistance and training, as well as members who may have money of their own to invest if your business purpose fits their social goals.

Should you go to each and every one of these organizations? No. You'd spend the next five years doing research and never get a business off the ground. Use the ideas here to focus on specific opportunities that fit your own profile. Perhaps you live in Kansas City. Then don't overlook the Marion Ewing Kauffman Foundation. Funded by the founder of a pharmaceutical company, this foundation's $1 billion purpose is to foster entrepreneurship in that area. Likewise, if your business focus is teenage girls, the incubators for young entrepreneurship may find your work worthy of support.

While you're reading about these specialized sources of training, information, and capital, think about similar local organizations that may be waiting in your own backyard.

Programs Specifically Targeting Women Business Owners

The Center for Policy Alternatives conducted a groundbreaking study that identified a critical component of women's business needs: the need for state support of women-owned businesses. While in the last chapter our focus was primarily on the federal level, here we look at specific state programs that provide—or fail to provide—support for women-led businesses.

STATES WITH MORE THAN 100,000 WOMEN-OWNED BUSINESSES

California	559,821
Texas	298,138
New York	284,912
Florida	221,361
Illinois	177,057
Pennsylvania	167,632
Michigan	133,958
New Jersey	117,373
Massachusetts	111,376

Source: National Women's Business Council, August 1995. In most cases, the states with the largest number of women-owned businesses have the largest concentration of programs for female entrepreneurs.

By surveying state economic development agencies and Small Business Development Centers (SBDCs), the Center for Policy Alternatives sought to uncover women's needs and areas where states could improve their delivery to women. Among other findings, the study found that "women entrepreneurs account for a smaller percentage of all state program users than the percentage of total business start-ups they represent...[M]any states do not implement useful programs to serve women-owned business [and] those states that do may not be reaching this target population... Women-owned businesses are generally smaller than male-owned businesses and, therefore, require special services tailored to their needs."

Recognizing that women have not had sufficient business access in the past, many government, university, and private agencies have started programs to increase women's business expertise. These programs typically combine training with counseling by experts. In some unique cases, they offer direct financing or access to financing. We'll look at some pioneer efforts that have set national and local standards.

American Women's Economic Development Corporation (AWED)

The American Women's Economic Development Corporation, a private, nonprofit corporation now entering its third decade, stands as the model for many of the newer efforts that have followed.

Conceived in 1976 by founder Beatrice Fitzpatrick to help women enter the world of entrepreneurship, the corporation helps women put their businesses on sound footing through services ranging from in-depth counseling and training programs to a hotline service.

When a business decides to enter an AWED, a major commitment by the entrepreneur of time and personnel resources is required. The meat of the AWED program is a four-month "managing your own business" course. This course serves women who have been in business for a year and generate at least $50,000 a year in business. AWED also offers two

> "AWED taught me how to run a business, not just a literary agency. I learned how to do a one-year and five-year plan and most importantly, a marketing plan to tie into the next year. This process brought focus to my work and therefore the specialities which have made my business a success—romance and finance."
>
> —Denise Marcil, Denise Marcil Literary Agency

educational sections: a "starting your own business" section featuring ten sessions for women considering becoming entrepreneurs, and an advanced business development roundtable for more experienced business women.

AWED operates in four cities—New York, Los Angeles, Washington, and Stamford, CT—and AWED-modeled programs operate in several more.

You can contact AWED through their hotline and telephone counseling number, 800-222-AWED; or in New York City at 71 Vanderbilt Avenue, New York, NY 10169. Phone 212-692-9100; fax 212-692-9296.

Women's Business Development Center (WBDC)

Hedy Ratner, codirector and cofounder of the Women's Business Development Center in Chicago, says she started her center in 1986 because "women need to find the resources to strengthen themselves in their own capacity to be better prepared." She felt the issues women must face are different: "Women have no assets; no property in their own names; small service businesses; no asset base; no access to networks; and they're not taken seriously by financiers, the government, or vendors." Ratner's purpose has been to change that in her own corner of the world with her business development center model.

WBDC LOANS

More than $1 million are loaned annually through the Women's Business Development Center's Women's Business Finance Program, with an average loan amount of $25,000.

Source: WBDC About Women's Business.

The center offers full-service business support services and is a national model for business innovation. Three critical programs form the backbone of the WBDC offerings: individual business consulting, entrepreneurial training, and access to capital for starting or expanding a business.

Among the training programs found at WBDC are entrepreneurial training; a twelve-week business development certificate; a "fast track" program to get women started who are not yet in business; and business workshops and conferences.

Capital programs include the Women's Business Finance program, a general financial consulting and access program; a microloan program that combines entrepreneurial training with a savings program for entrepreneurs who need loans of up to $5,000; and the Business Bank Loan Program, which provides established entrepreneurs with WBDC collateral loans between $20,000 and $50,000.

The Business Bank Loan Program includes consulting and workshops on financing. The fact that the loan committee is made up of bankers who want to do business with women entrepreneurs shows the real innovation at the Women's Business Development Center. The Women's Business Bank Loan Program demonstrates that if bankers want to find women entrepreneurs, they will find outreach opportunities such as this one to contact and cultivate the women-led business market.

The criteria for the loan program include:

- The business must be at least eighteen months old.
- The owner must have current financial statements.
- The business must show the ability to repay the loan.
- The owner's business and personal assets must secure at least 50 percent of the loan.
- The owner must have a positive personal credit history.

With the help of the SBA Office of Women's Business Ownership, the show has gone on the road. The program has expanded from the original locations in Rockford, Joliet, and Kankakee to Indianapolis, six cities in Ohio, Miami, and consultants in Boston and Philadelphia for starting up programs there. Hedy Ratner is also working to establish a national certification program for women's business development centers.

For further information, call 312-853-3477 or write Chicago Women's Development Center, 8 S. Michigan Avenue, Ste. 400, Chicago, IL 60603.

Microenterprise Loans

The concept of microenterprises, or very small businesses, has become a productive and popular concept around the world. In this country, microenterprising is hot, having recently been proposed as a way for women to work themselves out of welfare. In the fanfare, we mustn't overlook the small size of this loan program. If you need $100,000 or more, microloans aren't for you. But if your business is small and the difference between success and failure can be measured in the hundreds, then microloans make all the difference.

WOMEN'S SELF-EMPLOYMENT PROJECT (WSEPS)

Based in Chicago, the Women's Self-Employment Project focuses on microenterprise development, as do some sixty organizations nationally in the Coalition of Women's Economic Development.

While programs might focus on minorities, rural families, refugee families, or others, depending upon the needs of the community, here we'll focus on WSEP as a model for women business owners. Look in your own community, for these are community-driven programs, or contact one of the national groups or their branches.

WSEP offers a three-pronged approach: micro business development; microloans; and technical assistance and follow-up. In the mid-1980s WSEP was conceived by several concerned businesswomen in Chicago to

> **MICROENTERPRISING**
>
> A microenterprise is a very small business, often with one employee/owner, run from the home, and financed on a shoestring budget.

serve low-income women entrepreneurs in that city. WSEP has achieved several landmarks. It was the first group lending program for low-income urban women in the United States. WSEP's innovations influence other microenterprise programs around the country.

The women that WSEP serves typically come from households that they head, usually with children and without a second income. The WSEP customers are primarily women of color: approximately 85 percent are African American, 4 percent are Latina, and the remaining 11 percent are Caucasian.

The founder of WSEP, Connie Evans, grew up in Franklin, Tennessee, and watched her widowed mother work long hours as an independent caterer to feed and clothe four children. Her mother eventually was able to put Connie and her three siblings through private school and college. Today, Connie Evans helps other women with true grit like her mother reach their dreams. These women are

TRANSFERRING KNOWLEDGE ACROSS BORDERS

A group of Chicago business women studied one-person businesses in Bangladesh that were working well. The group founded WSEP based on their observations of Third World microlending programs. Now, WSEP's director, Connie Evans, serves as an advisor to the World Bank's microenterprise development program and advises the Rural Advice Center in South Africa on its economic development programs.

Source: *Chicago Tribune, 18 July 1993; Chicago Sun-Times, 12 March 1995.*

no different than many small business owners, and many success stories have started from one-woman, home-based operations. An African American herself, Evans is happy to blaze trails where few banks will follow. Many of the small businesses she helps fund, often microenterprises with revenues under $15,000 a year, will never see a commercial loan, but that doesn't mean that these businesses are insignificant to their owners or to the economy. One of the WSEP businesses is owned by a woman who began selling shoes as a public aid recipient. Now she runs her own store and her son, who is studying to be an accountant, keeps her books.

WSEP granted over $1 million to small women-led businesses in microloans in nine years.

Source: *Women's Self Employment Project, October 1995 Fact Sheet.*

When Evans started, there were fewer than ten microenterprise development programs in the country. Today the figure exceeds two hundred and is growing constantly. In fact, policy makers are now looking at microenterprise loans as a way to help women fund their way out of welfare.

For more information, contact Women's Self-Employment Project, 20 North Clark Street, Fourth Floor, Chicago, IL 60602. Phone 312-606-8255; fax 312-606-9215.

WOMEN'S INITIATIVE FOR SELF-EMPLOYMENT (WISE)

San Francisco's Women's Initiative for Self-Employment (WISE) program is typical of many microenterprise development/loan funds around the country. Considered a model for other programs, WISE is targeted to the specific needs of its community and limited to businesses in a specific five-county area. The program consists of two core business training workshops and a variety of supplemental topical seminars; only program participants may access the loan funds. If you live in the San Francisco area, seek out this program. If not, in looking for a similar organization be sure to check the combination of education, follow-up support, and funding. These three ingredients combined seem to be the key to the success of such programs.

Source: Women's Initiative for Self-Employment, 450 Mission Street, Ste. 402, San Francisco, CA 94105. Phone 415-247-9473; fax 415-247-9471.

While microenterprises aren't for everyone, and many women's needs far exceed microenterprise loan amounts, don't overlook these programs if you want to start small. If such microloan programs are available in your community, check them out. A microloan today could fund a successful venture on the NASDAQ tomorrow.

For information about microenterprise opportunities and loan funds in your area, contact The Association for Enterprise Opportunity (AEO) at 70 East Lake Street, Ste. 520, Chicago, IL 60601. Phone 212-357-0177; fax 312-357-0180. AEO is a national trade association of microenterprise development organizations.

The Aspen Institute

Long recognized as a top-notch think tank for national business leaders, the Aspen Institute has also entered the microenterprise field with its Self-Employment Learning Project (SELP). The project is designed to produce new information and encourage dialogue on the field of self-employment and microenterprise as a poverty-alleviation and employment-creation strategy. With that goal in mind, the Aspen Institute has produced a 150-page comprehensive directory of microenterprise projects around the country.

For information, contact Margaret Clark, Director, Self-Employment Learning Project, The Aspen Institute, Ste. 1070, 1333 New Hampshire Avenue, N.W., Washington, DC 20036. Phone 202-736-5800; fax 202-467-0790. The project publishes the valuable *Directory of Microenterprise Programs* (see "Resources and References" at the end of this chapter).

Individual Development Accounts (IDAs)

Individual Development Accounts (IDAs) function like Individual Retirement Accounts (IRAs) with a difference. Instead of funding retirement, their purpose is to provide economically deprived individuals with the hope of lifting them from welfare. So far, IDAs have only been sanctioned by legislation in four states and not at all on the federal level, but some proponents see them as models for potential federal action.

The IDA allows poor women on welfare to save in a special savings account that is excluded from asset calculations for the purpose of determining welfare eligibility. Depending on the state, the money is targeted for education, job training, or business start-up. The IDA interest is not taxed at the state level until it is withdrawn, and the state can provide matching funds.

Presently, four states offer IDA accounts:

- Arizona—solely for AFDC and food stamp recipients, IDA owners can use accounts only for college education or job training.
- Kansas—limited to saving for future education expenses for children of AFDC recipients.
- Mississippi—allows welfare recipients in the state's program to save money for medical expenses, college education, or retirement.
- Iowa—offers the most comprehensive program, which is available not only to welfare recipients but low-income individuals as well. Iowa matches a percentage of annual deposits with a "savings refund" of up to 20 percent from the state, depending on income.

With affirmative action in transition, programs that target selected groups that have a high proportion of women and minorities may offer politically palatable replacements to quotas. But in looking at any program that seeks to help women work off welfare, we mustn't lose sight of the fact that not everyone is cut out for entrepreneurship. Even among the non-welfare population, only a fraction of the labor force own their own businesses. To expect microenterprise or Individual Development Accounts to solve everyone's problems is to create unrealistic expectations.

For women who have zeal and the emotional ability to see beyond current barriers, these programs offer vision and hope. If you are a low-income potential entrepreneur, don't overlook these resources. With the help of training and funds, these programs can open the doors of opportunity.

If you live in any of these states or would like to find out more for starting such a program in your state, contact the Center for Policy Alternatives, 1875 Connecticut Avenue, N.W., Ste. 710, Washington, DC 20009; phone 202-387-6030. Ask for their report *State Support for Women-Owned Businesses*. The Center for Policy Alternatives is a nonprofit, nonpartisan group that promotes progressive public policy.

The Women's Network for Entrepreneurial Training (WNET)

The Women's Network for Entrepreneurial Training (WNET) matches successful entrepreneurial women (mentors) with women business owners whose companies are ready to grow. Meeting one on one over a period of one year, mentors guide new business owners through the process of achieving success in business. WNET is located within the Office of Women's Business Ownership at SBA.

The Women's Network for Entrepreneurial Training also provides a WNET Roundtable, which is a collaborative effort between the SBA Office of Women's Business Ownership and the SBA's Service Corps of Retired Executives.

Both mentors and protégés benefit from these programs. If, as a business-woman, you want a mentor, WNET requires that you have been in busi-ness for at least a year and be willing to spend a minimum of four hours a month with your mentor for a full year.

> Almost 950,000 small firms were assisted by the SBA in Business Education and Training in 1994.
>
> *Source: Small Business Administration, A Public/Private Partnership.*

Another Chicago-based group, the Illinois Women's Network for Entrepreneurial Training (IWNET), is one of the strongest WNET pro-grams in the country. Overseen by the Women's Business Advocate for the State of Illinois, Mollie Cole, IWNET has scored success after success with its mentor program. Like the other WNETs, IWNET is designed to assist small business owners by providing "linkages with other women entrepreneurs." Steel mill owners, electrical suppliers, and psychologists sing its praises. Funded as a cooperative endeavor between the Illinois Department of Commerce and Community Affairs and the Small Business Administration, the program contin-ues to serve as a model for others around the nation.

If you are interested in the WNET program in your area, contact the SBA OWBO at 409 3rd Street S.W., 6th floor, Washington, DC 20416. Phone 202-205-6673; fax 202-205-7287. Or ask for the Women's Business Owner representative in your local SBA office to learn if there is a WNET program in your state.

National Association of Women's Business Advocates (NAWBA)

The National Association of Women's Business Advocates comprises the women in state government responsible for representing women business owners in their states. These advocates are usually appointed by the governor of the state, but some are legislatively mandated. Program funding for these advocates comes from federal funds through the Small Business Development Center budget. In the present budget climate, advocates have to keep proving them-selves. Although the programs don't seem fully institutionalized and the women serve as volunteers, this group is committed to seeing women in business succeed.

NAWBA has no chapters and is not a membership organization. Rather, its mission is to provide an informal networking structure to exchange state by state information and share what programs do and do not work. Although the organization does no hands-on support for businesses, they work behind the scenes for policy changes and program development to support women-led businesses.

Currently, there are about twenty states with official NAWBA members. Those states have enacted Women's Business Ownership Acts or their equivalent. In addition to its current projects, NAWBA's long-term goals include the development of a national database of women business owners and the formation of a National Coalition of Women's Business Organizations.

For the individual woman business owner, the value of this group is twofold:

- If from your experience you have innovative programs or ideas for programs at the state level, communicate them to NAWBA.
- If you need to locate resources in your state, the NAWBA offices are well plugged in and can put you in touch with key people.

Although regular membership is reserved for state officials, any person who supports the goals of women's business ownership can join NAWBA as an associate member.

For more information, contact the National Association of Women Business Advocates, 100 West Randolph, Ste. 3-400, Chicago, IL 60601. Phone 312-814-7176; fax 312-814-2807.

Women's Business Development Councils

Women's Business Development Councils (WBDC) are advisory groups to the governor or legislature at the state level. They serve as informational clearinghouses, provide technical assistance, and act as a catalyst for networking among women-owned businesses. Though only a few states have such councils, they serve as an important resource in the states that do have them.

If you live in a state with such a council, look to it for information about business activities in your state and special programs of interest to women. The following are some of the most active Women's Business Development Councils:

- California Council to Promote Business Ownership by women, c/o Trade & Commerce Agency, 801 K Street, Ste. 1700, Sacramento, CA 95814-3520. Phone 906-622-7722.

- Colorado Women's Economic Development Council, c/o Women's Business Office, Economic Development Commission, 1625 Broadway, #1700, Denver, CO 80203. Phone 303-892-3840.
- Illinois Women's Business Ownership Council, Department of Commerce and Community Affairs, 620 East Adams, Springfield, IL 62701. Phone 312-814-7176.
- Women's Business Leadership Council, North Dakota Department of Economic Development and Finance, 1833 East Bismarck Expressway, Bismarck, ND 58504-6703. Phone 701-328-5300.
- Governor's Task Force on Businesses Owned by Women, Kentucky Cabinet for Economic Development, Capital Plaza Tower, 23rd floor, Frankfort, KY 40601. Phone 502-564-7140.

Women's Purchasing Council: An Experiment Worth Imitating

In New Mexico, leaders of the women's business community have inaugurated a purchasing council to increase the participation of women-owned businesses in corporate and government contracting at the city, state, and federal levels.

To achieve this ambitious goal, the Women's Purchasing Council has installed a vendor software program that will allow women-owned businesses to register as government vendors. Their registration will be shared with all participating government agencies.

Women own nearly a third of all small businesses in New Mexico, where the public sector makes up a large share of the economy with Air Force bases and research facilities. An increase in the number of public contracts with women-led businesses could make a tremendous difference for the some thirty thousand women-led businesses in the state.

For more information, contact New Mexico Women's Purchasing Council, P.O. Box 6706, Albuquerque, NM 87197-6706. Jan Zimmerman, Executive Director. Phone (505) 344-4230; e-mail: NMWPC1@aol.com.

Women Incorporated

Women Incorporated is a new organization for women entrepreneurs dedicated to aggregating the economic power of this rapidly growing constituency and improving their business environment. In early 1991, as the

"Given the dedication of women growing their businesses, it seemed remarkable and baffling that financial institutions would turn their backs on women."

—Judith Luther Wilder, cofounder of Women Inc.

founder of the California AWED, Women Inc.'s cofounder Judith Luther Wilder saw firsthand the problems women were having getting credit. Luther says she had "assumed women had a harder time getting capital and corporate discounts [for bulk purchases]," but she had no idea the extent to which women were simply cut out of the system. Luther says it became clear to her that "women needed more than they could get in the current marketplace."

Luther and her cofounder, Lindsey Johnson, the former head of the SBA Office of Women Business Ownership under the Bush administration, negotiated with The Money Store's CEO, Mark Turtletaub, to commit a $150 million loan pool for women-led businesses. According to Luther, Turtletaub "walked onto the limb with us," taking the risk of backing women-led businesses. Ironically, now that a major player has made such a commitment, Women Inc. has received much interest from other banks and institutions. Money talks—and a $150 million loan pool says a lot.

In fact, the $150 million represents almost a fourth of The Money Store's annual lending of $600 million in 1995. The Money Store is the biggest SBA lender in the country and has been the top such lender for the past twelve years. The Money Store has gone further to say the number is "not an absolute." If more qualified women apply for loans than this pool represents, The Money Store will increase its commitment.

"The Money Store is making a statement of our commitment to Women Incorporated and to women business owners."

—Carolyn Haught, The Money Store, commenting on the $150 million loan pool granted to Women Inc. by The Money Store

The lending criteria for Women Incorporated will be more flexible than that of The Money Store. Using a combination of SBA funds and traditional funding, Women Incorporated will lend to start-up businesses but prefers those with two to three years' experience. Instead of real estate or equipment collateral, the criteria will focus on cash flow, character, and training, whether by AWED or another technical assistance provider.

Women Incorporated is more than just a lending operation. With a goal of 1 million members, Women Incorporated is positioning itself as a force to be reckoned with. Already, Women Inc. has negotiated member discounts on business products and services with several large corporations, including AT&T, Kinko's, Northwest Airlines, and Federal Express. In contrast to NAWBO, with whom the new group is cooperating, Women Inc. will not have local chapters or training. Instead, they will refer women to existing training programs. Women Incorporated also provides a magazine, member newsletter, and educational publications, including "The Busy Woman's Guide to Successful Business Planning."

For more information or to join, contact Women Incorporated, 1401 21st Street, Ste. 310, Sacramento, CA 95814. Phone 800-930-3993 or 916-448-8444; fax 916-448-8898.

Legacies of the Capital Circle

In the booming women's business arena, many other groups are making attempts to get started to offer networking, training, and capital access. One such group, the Capital Circle, formed to bring together female investors and entrepreneurs from around the nation, stalled in its efforts. Nonetheless, through the Capital Circle's network, several initiatives have emerged and several strategic alliances have been built:

- A Harvard MBA is trying create an information group.
- A former bank officer is starting a consulting firm in the field.
- Former Capital Circle members who overlap with the Investors' Circle have an investor interest group that encourages the presentation of women-led deals at the Investors' Circle venture fair (see Chapter 4).
- A group of Capital Circle women met with the leadership of the Hollywood women's community to share information and ideas about capital.

All of these efforts are bound to reap large dividends, even if the underlying organization's ambitions did not survive the realities of the marketplace. The Capital Circle's membership dues were originally high—$1,000 a year—and the goals of the membership were sufficiently ambitious that one organization was hard put to contain them.

The experience of the Capital Circle also illustrates the many barriers to making capital more available to women. Women have needed capital for so long that the desire to quickly attain their goals almost overwhelmed this organization. The leaders have since pulled back to reexamine future directions.

To find the nearest women's organization or the national organization that relates to your business, refer to the Business Women's Network Directory at 800-48-WOMEN.

Training and Counseling for Entrepreneurs

Many entrepreneurial development programs are available across the country. They are designed to provide small business owners, whether planning for a new venture or already operating one, with the information and education to succeed.

TRAINED FROM THE START

Joline Godfrey, An Income of Her Own, Burbank

What do a female gang member, teen mother, and privileged prep school student have in common? "If they're girls, they're at economic risk," says Joline Godfrey, founder and director of the nonprofit organization that facilitates economic literacy in young women. An Income of Her Own sprung from Godfrey's realization that "with the feminization of poverty . . . we know there's something wrong with the way we're preparing girls and women for their economic well-being . . . and it's clear that if women are going to have strong healthy businesses we've got to start preparing them at an earlier age."

Her own entrepreneurial story exemplifies a pattern followed by many women, who tend to enter into business ownership only after they've gained a degree of success working for someone else. She points out, "Getting the self-confidence that says, 'I have what it takes to be the boss' is a very difficult process." Building this self-confidence is the core of AIOHO programs, which "reach across race, culture, and class."

AIOHO's diverse learning opportunities include day-long conferences to build awareness; an annual National Teen Business Plan Competition; Camp $tart-Up!, an eight-day skill-building residential summer camp; school programs such as satellite broadcasts on MCET and outreach for teacher–student participation; and support materials such as on-line services, games, videos, newsletters, and books. Making the materials and curricula available to other organizations is important to Godfrey, who is "not interested in building still another Girl Scouts or Girl's Inc." Instead, she hopes to partner with these and other girls' organizations to "provide yet another dimension for developing girls."

AIOHO's future includes a growing presence on the information superhighway via on-line services and Internet access because "unless girls are present on-line we're quickly going from economic haves and have-nots to the information haves and have-nots." Godfrey doesn't want to see girls left behind any longer. Her latest book, *No More Frogs to Kiss; 99 Ways to Give Economic Power to Girls* (New York: HarperCollins, 1995), is a testament to this cause. Her earlier book, *Our Wildest Dreams: Women Entrepreneurs Making Money, Having Fun, Doing Good* (HarperCollins, 1992) remains a classic.

Small Business Development Centers (SBDCs)

The SBA offers a Small Business Development Center Program, legislatively mandated by Congress in 1980, to act as consultants to small businesses on managerial and technical matters. SBDCs offer one-stop assistance to small businesses by providing information and guidance. The program is a cooperative effort involving the federal government, state and local governments, and the educational community. Most SBDCs are set on university campuses, where they can draw on the rich resources available in the academic environment to give practical help to businesses. The SBA has also partnered with private enterprises to form Business Information Centers, which work the same way as SBDCs.

Federal funding accounts for about half the SBDC budget, with sponsors providing the rest. SBDCs offer a variety of workshops to help you with your business. In a single month, the workshops in one SBDC location included the following:

- Cash Flow Forecasting for Small Businesses
- How to Get New Customers: Direct Mail for the Small Business
- Trademarks, Copyrights, and Patents
- How to Prepare a Business Plan
- How to Buy and Start the Right Franchise Business
- How to Start Up Your Own Business
- How Demographics Shape Export Strategies and Marketing
- Small Business and the Law
- How to Finance a Small Business
- How to Choose a Computer-Based Accounting System
- Marketing Your Product or Services
- How to Start a Consulting Business

During another month, the same center offered "Starting Your Own Business as a Woman Entrepreneur." (Unfortunately, the flyer was printed on pink paper. When will the color be retired from women-oriented affairs?) All of these offerings—a virtual mini-MBA in small business—cost $10 each.

Most SBDC locations also offer the free use of a computer complete with a laser printer for use in writing business plans. You could also choose from the "brown bag video series," which rotates topics such as speaking accounting, reading financials, and building budgets, or you can use the library of books and videos at the center.

From these materials, a second purpose of these centers becomes evident—the center gives you an opportunity to share with other businesspeople who may have similar problems and creative solutions. It is a good place to find moral support.

Contact the SBA Business Answer Desk at 1110 Vermont Avenue N.W., Washington, DC 20005. Phone 800-8-ASK-SBA; fax 202-205-7064. See the appendix for a national list of Small Business Development Centers.

The Service Corps of Retired Executives (SCORE)

The SBA's SCORE program aims to provide instant senior management without the cost. By connecting retired and senior executive volunteers with business owners and managers, the SCORE program offers management training, counseling, and advice. The program is available to any small business owner, and you can participate without an SBA loan or other relationship to the SBA.

If you feel you could use some free help, whether with an ongoing business or start-up, check out this program, which has operated successfully since 1964.

SCORE can be contacted directly at 202-205-6762, or you can reach them through your nearest SBA office.

Business School Entrepreneurship Programs

If you live near a major business school, don't overlook business school entrepreneurship centers as a source of information, training, and even capital connections. Most business schools have student projects that may loan you an MBA student for a semester—great for consulting and business plans writing. For example, at the University of Southern California, the entrepreneurship training program includes an internship with a business. And at the nearby UCLA Anderson School of Management, field studies require student teams to each study a business in depth for a year, with reports and presentations being the final product. A team of students will comb through the business or ambitiously research new markets, and the teams often include students with a variety of skills in finance, marketing, and accounting, as well as the legal, technology, retail, and entertainment fields.

Many business school entrepreneurship programs also offer management development programs for outside entrepreneurs. These programs may focus on assisting minority entrepreneurs or new managers of family businesses by connecting the small business owners with MBA student consultants. Although the initial engagement may be temporary, if you find good help through the program, longer-term projects can be arranged individually with the students.

The annual "Moot Corp" competition produces student business plans around the country, which are then judged in a national competition. The Students for Social Responsibility also hold a business plan contest. Both these efforts ultimately lead to prizes for the winners and exposure to capital. If you have a smashing business idea and can capture the attention and imagination of a business student, don't overlook the opportunity that working together on a business plan can provide both of you. MBA students have hot ideas, but they don't always have the connections to carry them off. If you have spent some years cultivating a community, hook up with a talented student to leverage both of your careers.

Contact your nearest business school for management interns or entrepreneurship programs.

Incubators

Business incubators operate like baby incubators in hospital nurseries—several baby businesses are gathered together in one place and a team of "nurses" and "doctors" (in the form of business advisors) help the baby businesses past their critical early days.

Many incubators are actual physical facilities. For example, a factory might be partitioned off into several small manufacturing sections, each an independent company, but they all might share administrative services and office space. In addition, the companies might receive help in the form of technical support or other services.

Another incubator example involves venture capital firms that have gathered ventures they are sponsoring under one roof. These companies provide budding entrepreneurs with office space and equipment, lawyers, bookkeepers, and the business advice needed to get funding for a new product. Among the active incubators are Mayfield Fund, Kleiner Perkins Caulfield & Byers, Merrill Pickard Anderson & Eyre, and Onset Enterprise Associates. About 3 percent of the total venture funding in 1993—$700 million—went into these incubators.

BUSINESS CONSTRUCTION: A COMPANY IN AN INCUBATOR

Pam Tucker and Nancy Showers, Utility Composites, Inc., Austin

When Pam Tucker and Nancy Showers entered the construction industry with their product line of plastic composite nails called Raptor, they were met with the same initial resistance by the male-dominated trade as were Connie Best and Sophia Collier in the beverage industry. Even though Pam held a Ph.D. in chemical engineering and Nancy had a successful marketing background with her own service company, they were still referred to as "the girls with the nails" at industry trade shows. But that attitude has changed as the women continue to earn the credibility and respect of their peers.

Pam and Nancy started Utility Composites, Inc. with the entirety of their savings. But just when things began to look promising, they began to run out of the initial $85,000 in start-up capital. They made a private offering for $400,000 but only raised $125,000, and a year later they were again in dire straits.

They began making presentations to raise an additional round of financing. During one presentation, a viewer suggested they approach the Austin Technology Incubator. They submitted a business plan and were accepted into the program by the selection committee after an interview with the program director.

The incubator proved to be more helpful than they had imagined. Although they had less space than they would have liked, the entrepreneurs were charged lower rents and did not have to sign a lease. They also were able to participate in a group health package and had the option of using a shared receptionist and office equipment. Mentoring was also available through the program in the form of informal advice by the program directors and other entrepreneurs in the program, as well as formal seminars given through the incubator for a nominal fee.

The greatest benefit of the program came unexpectedly for Pam and Nancy. Once they were admitted, they received instant publicity and credibility because of the incubator. An "angel" appeared who became the company's chief financial officer and 30 percent partner in return for his $300,000 investment.

As a businessperson, you should recognize that such underwriting of your overhead is capital. Having someone cover your overhead places you several steps up on the ladder of success. Seeing other businesses develop and having steady access to the management skills of the people who run the incubator gives you another boost.

Incubators expect their fledgling companies to graduate as financially viable businesses within two to three years.

Incubators aren't for everyone and they are location-specific, but if you are interested in finding out more, contact the National Business Incubation Association in Athens, Ohio, at 614-593-4331.

INCUBATORS FOR TEENS AND GIRLS

Though on the surface, incubator programs for girls and young women might seem far afield if your immediate goal in obtaining cash now, looking at these programs serves two purposes. First, they are true incubators of women-led businesses. Today's teens will be tomorrow's entrepreneurs, and if girls show an interest in entrepreneurship, they should be directed. Second, all of these programs have been funded by corporations and foundations that take an interest in women's businesses. They are good potential resources for your own training programs and even for direct sales. A number of these programs have gained national prominence.

Institutional Investors

Big money comes from big places. Pension funds, foundations, and large corporations all hold huge amounts of investment capital. In the past, because the funds were earmarked for retirements, charitable programs, and working capital, the investments made were extremely "safe"—that is, no venture capital investments. Recently, the tide is shifting, partly because the pension laws have changed, partly because the flow of venture capital investments has become more visible and favorable, and partly because the need for extremely conservative investing has waned.

Pension Funds

Pension funds hold in excess of 30 percent of all U.S. financial assets, according to the Federal Reserve Board. To understand the size of pension funds, consider:

YOUTH PROGRAMS

The following youth organizations tend to vary greatly in what they offer on a local level, but it's worth a call to the local chapter to inquire about business readiness or mentoring type programs. Look in the yellow pages under "Clubs and Organizations," or in the business section of the white pages.

An Income of Her Own
1804 West Burbank Boulevard
Burbank, CA 91506
800-350-2978

Programs range from day long AIOHO Conferences to an entrepreneurial summer camp called Camp $tart-UP! to a National Teen Business Plan Competition advertised through teen magazines. Materials and curricula that foster self-confidence and economic literacy in young women can be purchased for use by individuals or organizations.

Girl Scouts of the USA
420 Fifth Avenue
New York, NY 10018
212-852-6548

Famous for instilling leadership values in girls and women, Girl Scouts worked with the Ms. Foundation to originate the National Take Your Daughter to Work Day. Junior Girl Scouts (grades 4 to 6) may earn a Business-Wise Badge by designing their own business plan and completing related tasks. Cadette and Senior Scouts (grades 7 and up) may earn an Interest Project Entrepreneurship Badge by completing more in-depth activities aimed at honing entrepreneurial skills and awareness.

Girls Incorporated National Resource Center
441 West Michigan Street
Indianapolis, IN 46202
317-634-7546

Operation Smart encourages girls and teens to go into the fields of science, math, and relevant technology. Other programs foster positive life-enhancing qualities in girls and teens.

Junior Achievement Incorporated
800-843-6395

Volunteers visit elementary through high school classrooms to teach Business Basics and other related curricula. Additionally, many local chapters offer an extracurricular program for high school students in which the youth actually organize and operate their own business under the guidance of volunteer advisors from local businesses.

Young Women's Christian Association (YWCA)
726 Broadway
New York, NY 10003
800-YWCA-USA-1 (800-992-2871)

Program offerings include office/business skill training and a connection with Department of Labor's Job Corps.

- Pension funds are second only to corporate earnings as the largest domestic holdings.
- Pension funds hold more money than all of the personal savings accounts in the United States.
- In 1992, pensions invested more than $1 trillion.

With these numbers, women want a piece of the action.

There are two types of pension funds: public and private pension. Public pensions include state and local government employees' funds.

> "Public pension funds are more responsive than private funds because public pension funds are tax-driven bodies which derive their mandate from government and the public."
>
> —*Xcylur Stoakley, venture capitalist, Ark Capital Management*

Long a stronghold of safe investing because they represent the retirement savings of workers, pension funds have started to break out of their conservative confines.

Previously, with the passage of the Employee Retirement Income Security Act (ERISA), pensions were required to exercise their fiduciary duty with care to protect retirement income. As a result of this legislation, pensions tended to focus on the most conservative investments as a way to ensure financial stability. That act also prohibited trade-offs of return for social goals. Because many investment managers aren't familiar with social investing and do not realize that actual returns are often equal to or even better than social returns, the result has been a general taboo against "social" investing, which also included women- and minority-led businesses.

That landscape is changing with the creation of economically targeted investments (ETIs). This presidential executive order would allow pensions to dedicate a portion of their funds to investments offering positive returns but also in economically underserved investment areas, including women- and minority-led businesses. Unfortunately, according to venture capitalist Xcylur Stoakley, the tendency quickly developed to view ETIs as nonproductive investment giveaway sacrificing social goals for financial return.

Opponents to this direction have introduced legislation entitled the Pension Protection Act, which would prohibit pension plans from making economically targeted investments.

Even without these legislative mandates, pension funds have begun to turn to alternative investments. According to *Forbes* magazine, as stock and bond markets become more volatile, pensions look to the private capital marketplace. In 1993, $13 billion was invested in venture capital, leveraged buyouts, and other private deals. Returns are part of the attraction, according to *Pensions & Investments*. In 1992, the stock market produced a 7.7 percent rate of return, while venture produced an average 13.9 percent rate of return.

U.S. PUBLIC PENSION FUND INVESTMENTS

Only 0.6 percent of public pension fund investments are in small business.

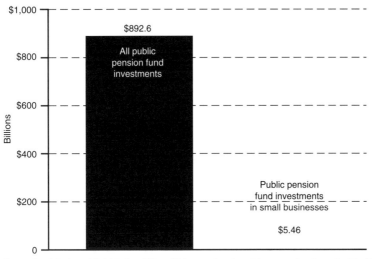

Source: Small Business Administration, Office of Advocacy, based on data prepared under contract by M & R Associates, Inc.

Small business activists at the 1994 White House Conference on Small Business were quick to point out that considering the size of federal pension holdings, pension investments to date are a drop in the bucket. At the conference, small businesses called for government pension funds to double their investments, noting that such an amount, while still only 2 percent of pension funds, would also double the venture capital marketplace!

For more information on ETIs, contact the U.S. Department of Labor, Pension and Welfare Benefit Programs, Office of Communications, 200 Constitution Avenue, Washington, DC. Phone 202-219-8784.

HOW TO GET MONEY FROM PENSION FUNDS

Despite the positive policy context, getting the money from pensions may prove difficult. Not only is the investment marketplace fairly invisible, like that for charitable and foundation investments, but pensions have shied away from investing in small businesses. Yet, some creative entrepreneurs have set out to get pension money and met with success.

Two women who have been quite successful in getting pension money invested in women-led and other small businesses are Margaret Fisher and Sona Wang of Inroads Capital Partners. Inroads, a women-led venture capital firm, has raised $40 million from pensions to date, including CALPERS (the California state employee pension fund), the St. Louis Teachers pension fund, the Illinois State Board of Investment public pension fund for state employees, and LaSalle National Bank. The two are continuing to approach institutional investors to reach their goal of raising $50 million to $75 million. Both women were trained in the traditional VC arena. They are looking for later-stage-companies with $10 million or more in revenues to place their investments.

For information, contact Margaret G. Fisher, Principal, Inroads Capital Partners, 1603 Darlington Avenue, Ste. 2050, Evanston, IL 60201. Phone 708-864-2000; fax 708-864-9692.

Another player is Xcylur Stoakley, an African-American entrepreneur who is raising $50 million for his venture fund, Ark Capital Management. Stoakley has substantial commitments from pension funds.

Ark has a general investment focus with emphasis on opportunities with women and minority-led companies. While the fund prefers later-stage oriented, middle market business as (companies with revenues of $5–10 million and growth prospects), they haven't closed the door to any firm.

Contact Xcylur Stoakley, Principal, Ark Capital Management, 150 North Wacker Drive, Ste. 2650, Chicago, IL 60606. Phone 312-541-0330; fax 312-541-0335.

Finally, JoAnn Price, formerly the head of the National Association of Investment Companies (NAIC), has put together $200 million in pension monies in order to fund minority enterprises. She used her contacts as a former administrator of a minority venture capital organization to create her own venture fund using pension monies.

Look to the public pension funds in your own state. Many of these funds set aside a portion of their money for local investment.

Remember, not all businesses will fit the pension profile. But also remember, not all women-led businesses are risky. If your business has a track record and you are thinking of expanding but need a large infusion of capital, the pension world deserves a close look.

More than 40 percent of all women-owned businesses have been in operation for more than twelve years.

Source: NWBC, Federal Reserve Bank, 3 June 1994.

Foundations

All foundations have *investment* programs. Many also have *grant* programs. Many businesses have been initially funded with grants from both charitable and business foundations.

Traditional multipurpose foundations have a deplorable track record for giving money to women. Funding for women's programs from foundations stands at a low 3.4 percent, hardly an encouraging record for entrepreneurs desiring to approach foundations for assistance. Two key groups are trying to remedy that situation: The Ms. Foundation for Women and the Women's Funding Network.

Both these efforts are based on value systems that emphasize increasing the amount of funding for women's projects, encouraging women to become donors to women, and working to build links across class and race.

THE MS. FOUNDATION

The Ms. Foundation is the largest foundation in the United States specifically devoted to women. The foundation was conceived during the early years of *Ms.* magazine by founders Gloria Steinem and Pat Carbine. Over the years, the foundation, now headed by President Marie Wilson, has been a leader for innovation in programs directed to women.

> Although the number of women and children in poverty has climbed to more than 75 percent of the nation's 32 million poor, foundation funding for programs for women and girls, as a share of all foundation funding, grew from 1981 to 1987 by only 0.5 percent.
>
> Source: Angela Bonavoglia, "Far From Done: The Status of Women and Girls in America," A Survey of Needs and Resources, 1980–1990. Published by Women and Philanthropy, New York.

Though its programs do not target business ownership specifically, as an informal clearinghouse and a general source of information for women, the Ms. Foundation must be included in any businessperson's short list of information sources. The foundation also has put together a collaborative program with the Ford Foundation, the John D. and Catherine T. MacArthur Foundation, the McKay Foundation, and many other philanthropic leaders. Called the Collaborative Fund for Women's Economic Development, these foundations are each contributing to women's economic development. Fifteen job-creation organizations have benefited so far in the effort to help stabilize women's microenterprises.

The director of the Economic Development Program, Sara Gould, emphasizes that the nine-year effort doesn't give money directly to low-income women, but focuses its efforts on capacity-building for women's nonprofits who serve these women, especially with microenterprise promotion. Part of the collaborative effort involves training in the annual Institute on Women and Economic Development, which is aimed at providers. We are "trying to achieve a more effective provision of capital to low-income women by strengthening intermediaries. This work is important because so much entrepreneurial talent among low-income women is being missed out on for lack of small amounts of equity."

Finally, Gould points out that microenterprise will not solve the problems of the entire welfare system, but for the right women, the program can bring great success.

This truly remarkable $2.2 million effort, conceived by the Ms. Foundation, is worth your attention if you are a woman who fits the profile of the targeted group, low-income women or women of color (or if you've made money and are ready to share it).

For information, contact The Ms. Foundation, 120 Wall Street, 33rd Floor, New York, NY 10005. Phone 212-742-2300; fax 212-742-1653.

WOMEN'S FUNDING NETWORK

Like the mission of the Ms. Foundation, the Women's Funding Network (formerly the National Network of Women's Funds) focuses its attention in the nonprofit area. The mission of the network is to promote the development of women's funds that empower women and girls, encouraging cooperation across race and ethnic or economic class lines. The network works with the 80 plus women's funds around the country that focus exclusively on empowering women in all areas, including business development and training.

MOVING CAPITAL

Tracy Gary, Resourceful Women, San Francisco

Where do you go if you're a women with at least $25,000 in discretionary income from your earnings or inheritance but don't feel confident managing it? Where can such "well-endowed" women find education, support, and empowerment to channel their money into positive social change? Tracy Gary, founder of a San Francisco–based nonprofit group called Resourceful Women, says it is the only resource center of its kind in the U.S. Tracy Gary finds that "Learning about money—managing it, talking about it with loved ones, using it to bring about social change—is as important for women today as it was for our mothers to learn to drive and our grandmothers to secure the right to vote."

While it's important to realize that this group is not a grant-making organization, its membership rolls represent some of the wealthiest women in the U.S. With a mission to "inspire social activism and informed philanthropy," many of their investment dollars are channeled directly into women-owned business through seed grants or indirectly through community loan funds.

Gary likes to dispel the myth that socially responsible investing means low returns. Since 1973 she has "had 100 percent of her money in socially responsible investments and a tremendous partnership with community-based businesses, netting an 11 percent return when the general investment market has averaged only 10 percent." She adds that, whatever their means, "women need to think wholistically about their economic empowerment and literacy." Members are treated to a variety of learning forums, from money management basics to education about specific social issues for investment purposes. For more information see "Resources and References" at the end of this chapter.

For information, contact Carol Mollner, Women's Funding Network, 1821 University Avenue, Ste. 409N, St. Paul, MN 55104-2801. Phone 612-641-0742; fax 612-742-1653.

THE KAUFFMAN FOUNDATION SEED CAPITAL FUNDS

One foundation in particular may deserve your attention because of their unusual entrepreneurial program. The Ewing Marion Kauffman Foundation of Kansas City was set up in the early 1990s with the specific mission of furthering entrepreneurship and youth development. Endowed with $1 billion by pharmaceutical entrepreneur Kauffman, the foundation restricts grant-making to partnerships and collaborations with other nonprofit, tax-exempt organizations.

One special project, the seed capital funds, will be of interest to women and minority business owners in Kansas City and the surrounding region. The parent Kauffman Foundation has set aside $1 million each for three seed funds: The Seed Capital Fund for Women, the Seed Capital Fund for Hispanics, and the Seed Capital Fund for African Americans. These funds are administered by the Center for Business Innovation, and investment decisions will be made by three separate investment committees with representatives of each targeted community.

If you are in the Kansas City area, contact the seed funds at the Center for Business Innovation, 4747 Troost, Kansas City, MO 64110. Phone 816-561-4646. If you have a nonprofit training organization and you are interested in applying to the Kauffman Foundation or other foundations, see *The Foundation Directory* in your local library or call The Foundation Center at 212-807-3600. Review the individual foundation's criteria to see which fit your area of activity.

WHY FOUNDATION WORK IS VITAL

A former member of the Ms. Foundation staff, Iva Kaufman, captured the essence of what all the microenterprise and foundation collaborative work is about: "How to create the kinds of programs that nurture proximity between women across class. Fundamentally unless we build relationships between women who have resources and women who need resources, there's no synergy for women to invest in women-owned businesses. Women who have access to money don't understand how a few strategically placed investment dollars can change the lives of women in other communities. Operating with the upper-middle-class mind-set that you need a lot of money to start a business or stabilize a family or community, many women are not in touch with the creative alternatives their money, properly targeted, can do in low-income situations. We need to create more forums where women can interact with one another and understand what they can do for one another."

For a consultant on funders of community based organizations, contact Iva Kaufman Associates, 900 West End Avenue, #7B, New York, NY 10025.

Another observer points out that so far, the work with the population of women has been specialized around economic demographics. This astute student of the women's world sees the Ms. Foundation as primarily working with low-income women; AWED, with middle class; and the SBA, middle- and upper-class women. The need still exists to build relationships across class.

If your business would benefit from seed funding to develop a new idea or area, consider foundations as a point to explore. See the resource section for *The Foundation Directory*, the general starting place to review which foundations support what kinds of work.

Religious Organizations

Religious organizations are another group interested in progressive social change using investment funds to promote their point of view. Most of the religious organizations, including churches, synagogues, and temples, have endowments that are invested reflecting their social values. Minority- and women-owned businesses are two of the target groups that can benefit from these funds.

> "The alternative investment dollars available from religious based loan funds are not for everyone, especially not for those looking for venture capital. This money is generally targeted to businesses and community development programs that are already serving the local community in a meaningful way."
>
> —Tim Smith, executive director of the Interfaith Center on Corporate Responsibility (ICCR)

For information about religious investments in community economic development, contact Gary Brouse, Director of the Interfaith Center on Corporate Responsibility's Clearinghouse of Alternative Investments, 475 Riverside Drive, Room 566, New York, NY 10115. Phone 212-870-2316.

Large Corporate Grants and Investment

Almost all of the Fortune 500 companies as well as many other lesser-known corporations have special investment programs funded by a small portion of the corporations' surplus working capital. Most of the excess cash is used to invest in other corporations and government bonds; however, the set-asides are typically many times the size of your financing needs.

Typically, the corporation will designate an agent who specifically deals with corporate charitable and other funding requests. Many

A CALL FOR CAPITAL

Rebecca Maddox: Capital Rose, Inc., Pennsylvania

Many of the women featured in this book were visionaries in the early days of the women-owned business movement. They saw, tracked, and set the trends. When corporate reality had not quite caught up with their visions, they tenaciously persevered.

As senior vice-president of marketing in a large diversified financial services company, Rebecca Maddox was one such woman. In 1990 she responded to what she identified as "the power and impact of the women-owned business market" by creating a subsidiary company called Compass Rose Development Corporation. Its mission was to educate women about the ins and outs of business ownership. After participating in the educational component, women could apply for financial packages through a sponsoring parent company. Although it was widely acclaimed as a success in the media, the corporate sponsor terminated the program in 1993.

Out of the ashes, a handful of women came together to form Capital Rose, a for-profit consulting firm working with Fortune 500 companies to dispel marketing myths about women. As director of advocacy Jean Brooks jokes, many of their corporate clients are surprised when they learn that "they can't just make it pink and put a bow on it" to attract women.

While their behind-the-scenes consulting work is admirable, Capital Rose has a greater mission in its not-for-profit Capital Rose Perpetual Fund. Rebecca Maddox conceived the idea for the $40 million loan fund, which is self-supporting by reinvesting proceeds from interest. Capital Rose hopes to fill a niche for women seeking loans between $50,000 and $1 million, reasoning that smaller loans are available through microlending programs and larger ones would be covered in the venture capital markets. The fund was officially started in 1995, when Rebecca Maddox put out calls for women across America to contribute $10 each. The women at Capital Rose feel that most people can write a check for $10 without the decision-making process that a larger donation would entail. Capital Rose will begin making loans when the fund reaches $10 million.

As Capital Rose grows, the founders will add new financial products and services targeted to women business owners. For example, the firm is currently looking for ways to make 401K plans more accessible to small businesses that traditionally can't handle the exorbitant start-up costs. They are also determining alternative structuring for mortgage products that would allow for the differences in income stream characteristic of self-employed women.

In addition, Rebecca Maddox authored *Inc. Your Dreams* (Penguin, 1995) to "provide as many women as possible with a process for examining what they love to do and making a commitment to doing it" while helping them determine whether business ownership is right for them.

Whether you'd like to contribute to the perpetual fund, apply for a loan, or inquire about the activities of Capital Rose, please contact Capital Rose, Inc., Attn: Jean Brooks, 690 Sugartown Road, Malvern, PA 19355. Phone 610-644-4212; fax 610-644-4748; e-mail: CRoseInc@aol.com.

not-for-profit companies have found financing success through this route. For example, a poetry publisher may recognize that publication costs will probably exceed revenues, especially when you take her salary into account. Rather than constantly struggle for profits, the publisher can set up a not-for-profit publishing house and appeal to local corporations for funding.

Why would corporations make grants to such endeavors? Aside from the philanthropic importance of such support, the corporations recognize a secondary benefit—good PR. Corporations strive to maintain good relations with their shareholders, employees, and the public in part by showing their social responsibility. Even companies that are otherwise considered to be socially irresponsible, such as cigarette manufacturers, will have such grant programs in place.

At the other extreme, corporations will invest in other public companies to spread out their investments. If you plan to take your company public, institutional investors can be crucial to the success of your initial public offering.

A listing of corporations that have formed alliances and joint projects can be found in Silver, *Venture Capital* (see "Resource and References," Chapter 4). Also, look in the business section of your local library. Most of these sections feature information about corporations in your area. In general, it's easiest to start with those nearest you because many times their corporate mission includes helping foster business development in their corporate backyards.

Private Sources of Policy Study and Information for Women Business Owners

Aside from the numerous governmental sources of information, private groups have focused their research efforts on women business owners.

National Foundation for Women Business Owners (NFWBO)
The most important source for research on women-owned businesses, aside from the SBA itself, is the National Foundation for Women Business Owners (NFWBO), the research and education arm of the National Association of Women Business Owners (NAWBO). NAWBO is a powerful and well organized networking, training, and advocacy group. Check out your local chapter. NFWBO supports the growth of women business owners and their organizations through gathering and sharing information. If you have an interest in locating nontraditional funding sources, NFWBO should be on your short list of places to call, along with the National Women's Business Council (see Chapter 4).

For more information on membership or research, contact the National Association for Women Business Owners or the Foundation at 1100 Wayne Avenue, Ste. 830, Silver Spring, MD 20910-5603. NAWBO phone 301-608-2590; fax 301-608-2596. NFWBO phone 301-495-4976; fax 301-495-4979.

Center for Policy Alternatives

The Center for Policy Alternatives in Washington, D.C., has also done research on various women's issues, including a study of business resources at the state level.

To obtain the study and other publications, or to ask about state resources, contact the Center for Policy Alternatives, 1875 Connecticut Avenue, N.W., Ste. 710, Washington, DC 20009. Phone 202-387-6030; fax 202-986-2539.

The Internet as a Business Tool

The Internet ("the Net") and World Wide Web (WWW or "Web") provide information access, potential location of capital, chat-rooms to visit with other entrepreneurs, e-mail, and conferencing facilities for the business owner. Because of its low cost and relatively easy use, the Web may be one of the most significant tools for the small-business person since the invention of the printing press. Most of the explosion of the Internet has come about since mid-1994, and the growth of new sites occurs at such a pace that the only way to see the potential is to get "on-line."

The World Wide Web is a part of—or protocol of—the vast interconnecting links of personal computers, "servers" (computers), and hosts (computer complexes) around the world called the Internet. The special capability of the WWW is its ability to deliver user-friendly graphics, audio, and video, as well as to "hyper-link," or connect, you to any site worldwide instantly with the click of a button.

In order to access or be able to "browse" and search the WWW, find a local or national Internet service provider (ISP) advertising web access and subscribe just as you would to phone service. Cost for unlimited monthly access stands at about $20 per month and with the entry of both ATT and MCI into the marketplace, prices can be expected to remain competitive. Since toll charges can drive up the cost of your usage, if your service doesn't provide a toll-free 800 number, make sure the company offers a local number toll-free to your telephone.

Don't confuse the WWW with America Online or Compuserv, two of the most prominent commercial services that offer prepackaged on-line information, as well as access to the Internet. These services provide many useful proprietary sources of information, including on-line versions of consumer and business publications, but you pay $2 to $3 an hour for your use. So, the best bargain for business people is to have a direct Internet connection through an ISP, as well as access to one of the commercial servers.

Don't be afraid to get on the Net and browse using keyword search capabilities provided by "search engines" such as Yahoo!, Lycos, Infoseek, Magellen, and Excite. These are built into Netscape, the dominant software provider, as well as into Microsoft Windows '95.

Just looking up "women" and "business," we turned up sites from the National Women's Business Council to the announcement of conferences and programs of interest to women entrepreneurs. In addition, you may find Women's Wire, a large site dedicated to women's concerns, a good place to start, as it's user-friendly to women.

Or, if like most businesses, you want to get the word out, consider building your own Web site. Site construction can run as low as a few hundred up to many thousand dollars, depending upon the complexity of your design. You'll also have the overhead of keeping a communications link to the Internet. See "Resources and References" for how to contact our site and information about how to build your own.

Staying Involved

Even if you don't need direct help from the organizations we've reviewed in this chapter, their policies and positions affect your business life. All women business owners must concern themselves with the environment in which their businesses operate. That environment affects all owners. If you need access to loans, if you are concerned about the future of federal programs, if you want to help assure that your state's budget includes helping women-led businesses, or if you want to give back to other women, these resources provide places to connect with other like-minded business owners.

When approaching foundations and pension funds, your efforts to get information will make them more sensitive to the needs and abilities of women business owners. Foundations have done surprisingly little to support and invest in women-led businesses as compared with grant programs, which are admittedly thin. Pensions funds, likewise, must be educated to include women-led businesses in their investment plans.

Resources and References

There are many associations and groups that offer training, assistance, and advice to the entrepreneur. Look at *The Business Women's Network Directory: Profiles of the Top 400 U.S. Business and Professional Women's Organizations, 1995–1996* (Washington, DC: The Business Women's Network, 1996) or the listing of the NWBC Women's Business Coalition (see appendix) to find groups that interest you.

The 1994 Directory of U.S. Microenterprise Programs. Order from the Aspen Institute, P.O. Box 222, Queenstown, MD 21658. Phone 410-820-5326; fax 410-827-9174. $15.

Feczko, Margaret Mary. *The Foundation Directory*. The Foundation Center, Columbia University Press, 17th ed., 1995.

Godfrey, Joline. *No More Frogs to Kiss: 99 Ways to Give Economic Power to Girls* (New York: HarperCollins, 1995). Excellent book for teenage women seeking economic empowerment, including entrepreneurial tips.

Resourceful Women, Presidio Building, #1016, P.O. Box 29423, San Francisco, CA 94129-0423. Phone 415-561-6520; fax 415-561-6462.

INTERNET RESOURCES

Women's Wire: http://womens.com

National Women's Business Council: http://www.sbaonline.sba.gov/womeninbusiness/wnetcov.html

SBA: http://www.sbaonline.sba.gov

Web Site Builders: NBO, 8306 Wilshire Blvd., Ste. 813, Beverly Hills, CA 90211; email: NBOWEB@aol.com

Business Capital for Women: http://www.womenmoney.com

Broadhurst, Judith A. *The Women's Guide to Online Services* (New York: McGraw Hill, 1996).

CHAPTER 6

Business Sources of Capital

Once your venture is operational, several additional sources of capital become available to your business. Many of the techniques in this chapter involve substantial trade-offs. In these cases, it would have been better to start up the company with sufficient working capital to meet the hard times. Nonetheless, the financing techniques below have been successfully used by new, healthy, and distressed companies alike.

Partnering

We usually think of "partnering" as referring to two individuals, but many companies have successfully partnered as well. Company partnering has become an increasingly widespread approach to business, for both financial and operational reasons. Your business may be well suited to enter into a joint venture with another company for any number of reasons.

Corporate Partners

Your corporate partner may be a company that can distribute your product. Your company, in turn, provides them with the exclusive right to distribute the goods. The same result can also be accomplished through a licensing agreement. Media companies typically gain financing and revenue through product and distribution agreements with other companies in the same industry. For example, often film producers presell foreign distribution rights to film distribution companies that want to show the movie abroad.

In other cases, your company supplies necessary goods or services to your (usually larger) partner. By partnering, your corporate partner ensures a steady stream of supplies or services. In return, you may get start-up financing and a bankable, stable revenue stream. Such an arrangement must be mutually beneficial to be effective. You get capital and your corporate partner gets serviced for presumably less money and fewer management hassles than bringing the operation in house.

Let's say Jane prints corporate stationery on a wholesale basis. Typically, her "markup" or profit as a wholesale stationery supplier is 40 percent. But Jane cuts a deal with Consolidated Electronics to supply all their paper for a 20 percent markup. In exchange, Consolidated provides access to its own lines of credit with suppliers of paper, ink, and printing equipment, including presses, cutters, and folders. Jane's company becomes financially solid even though profits arc lower. She has 100 percent collection on receivables and no finance charges to pay. Consolidated obtains its paper for 20 percent less and enjoys a steady supply without having to stock excess inventory, saving cash and storage space. Consolidated's cost of providing credit to Jane's company is marginal considering its large credit line. Consolidated ends up saving more than 20 percent on its paper costs while Jane increases her net profits and improves the financial condition of her company.

Licensing

You may decide to avoid taking on a business partner or raising additional capital by instead licensing the right to use your product to others. Often used by inventors, licensing enables you to rent your product to another company on a per-use basis. The licensee or person renting the product may negotiate the exclusive right to use the product but never owns the product. In this way, you can earn a steady cash flow from royalties and licensing fees without losing your creation through a direct sale of the company or your technology.

Video game manufacturers, such as Sega and Nintendo, have been especially effective in charging a licensing fee for every single video game cartridge sold for their systems.

Joint Ventures

One popular, and less intimidating, form of corporate partnering is the joint venture. Instead of agreeing to get married to a corporate partner, you agree to go on an extended vacation. You become involved in a specific project or venture for a limited period of time or for a limited purpose. Like a corporate partnership, a corporate joint venture is usually done between complementary companies, each contributing to a venture in a specific way.

PRINCIPLED PARTNERSHIP

Geeta Bhide, Walden Capital Management, Boston

By 1993, Geeta Bhide had worked in the corporate world long enough to "see what other people left for." Although she was comfortable in her prestigious job as senior vice-president of the United States Trust Company in Boston, she felt her lifetime dream of owning her own business was slipping away. When a mutual friend introduced her to Jay Bradgon, founder of Conservest Management Company, the seed was planted for a joint venture. Within a year, that seed had grown into Walden Capital Management, Geeta's answer to her need for "ownership, authorship, and freedom to work creatively" that she feels is missing from most employment situations.

In their joint venture, Jay retained ownership of Conservest, a pioneer in socially responsible investing. He provided start-up money, space, and staff support for Geeta's business, Walden Capital Management, in return for equity in her company. They both benefit from the relationship by sharing overhead costs such as workspace, equipment, and support personnel. For example, they are able to afford better workspace in a nicer building than they would if going it alone.

As in any successful joint venture, Geeta and Jay's services complement one another yet work on the same principles. They are equally concerned with socially responsible investing, but Conservest works mainly with family groups and Walden with institutional investors. Additionally, both recognized the need for international expertise and welcomed Brandywine Asset Management, an international investment firm based in Wilmington, Delaware, into their joint venture.

Geeta's advice? "It is important to have a good contract and a good business relationship before you let the lawyers in. Ultimately, there will be surprises, but pay attention to the chemistry between the principals [owners]. Everything rides on working together."

International Partnering

One increasingly attractive option given the constantly diminishing size of our planet is to recruit international partners. Opening your venture to the international scene vastly increases the pool of potential investors.

Some global regions are quite interested in female entrepreneurs. Other regions, such as South America, are extremely receptive to investment of any type and are supportive in arranging bank financing and other financial services.

> "Money is money. You can get that anywhere. But foreign intelligence—information about markets abroad—is regionally specific. Each is required to take your company abroad. And with an international partner, you get both."
>
> —*Merry Tuten, CEO, Greater Los Angeles World Trade Center Association*

But your international partners not only provide capital, they give you access to international markets. By providing current information about their local economies and consumers, you become equipped to expand to foreign soil.

Companies don't have to be huge to be international. Some multinational companies have actually been extremely supportive of very small companies in the United States. And the multinational corporations have been quite attracted by women-led companies, in some cultures because they are common, in others because they are so different.

So why have women been slow to take advantage of the global economy?

Inexperience.   Because women have been late entrants into the domestic business world, few feel sufficiently grounded to operate internationally. And many women feel their companies are too small or their management teams are too green to face international complications. The reality is, in many industries, women-owned businesses are facing international competition, even if the women keep their operations local. Even local clothing designers compete against European designers, and many goods come from India, Taiwan, and Korea.

In 1990, so few women business owners had gone overseas that the SBA began seminars specifically to encourage women to go international.

Discrimination.   In many parts of the world, women are still forced to wear veils and walk two steps behind men. These cultures have not been acculturated to accept female executives and business owners. But old barriers to women's international ventures are falling fast with faxes, telecommuting, the Internet, and government initiatives to protect women-business owners abroad.

Inconvenience.   The reality is, physical considerations still make going abroad difficult for women. Concerns about child care and physical safety (particularly from sexual assault) continue to make international business travel difficult for women on our slowly evolving planet.

Ironically, while U.S. women have been slow to discover the international marketplace, international lenders are targeting women abroad. The projects these women pursue—from selling charcoal to raising crops—have long been the backbone of Third World economies. "All over the developing world, in rural areas, women are the mainstay of the local economy," according to Gustave Speth, administrator of the United Nations Development Program quoted in the *Wall Street Journal*. In fact, in 1953, the so-called "market mammies" produced the strongest civilian resistance to colonialism since Gandhi's victory in India. By withdrawing consumer goods from the marketplace that they controlled, these determined women forced the British to leave Ghana, making that nation the first on the continent of Africa to attain home rule. While in most developing countries, women have been left behind by the process of modernization, many have strong indigenous cultures that respect women. When American women go abroad to do business, they should look to the local culture to find models as reference points for doing business.

Balance Sheet Financing

Once your company becomes operational, you should probably have collateral in the form of property, equipment, finished goods, raw materials or accounts receivable. Lenders thrive on collateral. They want to ensure their loans with property you put up. Banks and other financial institutions want to know that if you default, at least they can collect in some form. Some financial institutions take it one step further. Instead of using your receivables, inventory, or equipment as collateral for the loan, they actually buy the goods. You get the cash (at a premium), and they get the goods (at a discount).

Receivables Financing

Receivables financing or "factoring" is an extremely popular, and costly, way for distressed companies to raise cash. Factoring is the sale of your accounts receivable at a discount. The receivables can usually be sold to a specialty financing company, often at a deep discount. Factoring tends to be a

SOME QUICK ACCOUNTING
Receivables are moneys owed to you from sales made on account. Your accounts receivable are the bills you have sent out that have not been paid to you.
Payables are moneys owed by you to another. Your accounts payable are the bills you haven't paid yet.

financing technique of last resort; you will usually only earn about 75 percent on your accounts receivable (although this percentage varies depending on the strength of your accounts) because they may be difficult to collect. If you have a strong track record of collecting the cash due, this translates to a 25 percent price tag for early delivery of the cash.

You should consider factoring only if you absolutely cannot wait for your receivables to come through the door. Because retail and most service operations have few accounts receivable given the widespread use of personal credit cards today, factoring is best employed by manufacturers and wholesalers who tend to have a large amount of their sales sold on account.

Aileen was very successful, selling thousands of lounge chairs to retail stores and billing their accounts, but she still had no cash because the buyers had not paid. She was unable to speed up their repayment by calling or offering early payment discounts. She decided to factor her receivables. Although she had to sell the receivables at a discount, she got the cash she needed to keep her operation alive in the short term.

Be sure to consider the impact factoring may have on your customers. In many cases, the factoring company will collect the receivables directly from your accounts. In other words, your customers will know that you have factored your receivables because someone other than you is demanding payment. Depending on your relationship with your customers, this may or may not have an impact. If it will, consider negotiating the right to continue collecting yourself or rethink whether factoring is the right tactic for you.

Inventory Financing

Inventory financing is done primarily as part of your receivables financing package. Inventory is worth even less than receivables as collateral; usually only 50 percent of the value of the inventory is financed. The type of inventory capable of being financed is largely limited to finished goods. Raw materials are more difficult to finance.

> **ADDITIONAL COLLATERAL**
>
> Inventory can be used as additional collateral to negotiate a 100 percent financing of your receivables.

The financing source will often own the inventory financed until it is sold. Because the true value of your inventory is often difficult to determine, and some products risk quickly losing value or becoming obsolete, the institutions are rarely willing to consider more than 50 percent of the market value of your goods, despite your arguments to the contrary.

Equipment Financing

Equipment financing or leasing is available for almost any piece of new, and most pieces of used, equipment. Leases can be obtained directly from the equipment vendor or indirectly through a financial institution.

A typical lease requires a down payment and monthly rental fees. The interest rate and the final buyout price are typically negotiated depending on your credit, the length of the lease, and the value of the equipment at the end of the lease. Because of today's exponential rate of technological change, the value of the equipment at the end of the lease is often the most disputed component of the negotiations, particularly for long-term leases.

Leases are not limited to equipment that you need to buy. *Sale-leasebacks* enable you to sell your equipment to a financing company and then lease it back. In this way, you get the cash now and pay later. Of course, you pay a premium, in terms of interest and other transaction fees, for the benefit of the cash up front.

Cash Flow Management

Effective cash flow management can improve both the stability and profitability of any company, whether distressed or successful. Often, managers blindly leave the cash flow management to the accountants or their bookkeeping departments. In fact, they should apply the aggressive, entrepreneurial style responsible for marketing successes to bookkeeping.

Although tighter cash flow control may not solve all of your financing problems, improving your cash management could prevent the need for bridge financing, short-term loans, or equity capital to carry you through a short-term cash flow crisis.

PAYABLES MANAGEMENT

If you've ever found your personal finances in a tight spot, you know what "payables management" is. This fancy term describes the process of selectively timing your payment of bills.

If you have sufficient cash to do so, the early payment of payables usually results in substantial discounts. For example, you may earn a 5 percent discount for the immediate payment of supplies received. Too often, managers view this as a friendly discount.

Let's instead look at the discount as a 5 percent *penalty* if the supplies are not paid for in a timely fashion. If you buy $1,000 worth of supplies each month and are offered a 5 percent discount for payment within ten days of purchase, you can save $50 each month. Or put another way, you are penalized $600 a year for not paying early. By viewing the payment terms as involving a penalty that should be avoided, you can better account for this hidden cost of inefficient cash management.

At the other extreme, payables management is the single largest source of capital for most start-ups. If you don't have enough money to pay all of your suppliers, your natural reaction, aside from panicking, will be to determine which of your creditors you have to pay now and which you can pay later. For some entrepreneurs, this payables juggling act can last months or even years as they struggle to keep their companies alive. For undercapitalized companies, paying bills at the last minute and calling creditors daily becomes a way of business life.

In general, some creditors can wait sixty or ninety days for payment while others will require immediate payment. Even if you have no suppliers in the manufacturing or retail sense, tight cash flow could limit your ability to pay employees and utility bills. Should you find yourself in a payables juggling act, consider the following:

- Your tendency will be always to pay the most persistent creditors. As the saying goes, "the squeaky wheel gets the grease." Try to think through your payables management and stick to your strategy. It is dangerous to operate with the haphazard

**TRADE CREDIT: TIMING YOUR ACCOUNTS PAYABLE
DUE DATES AFTER YOUR SALES**

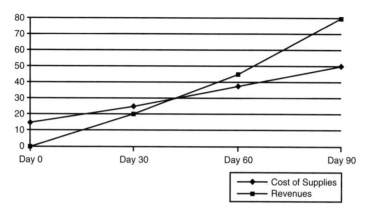

payment of your accounts due. The best strategy is to isolate your "bookkeeping" even if you are the bookkeeper yourself. Keep a separate voice mailbox for bookkeeping. Don't combine bookkeeping calls with sales calls, as your sales ability will be hampered if you have just fended off a creditor; instead, set aside a few hours each week dedicated exclusively to bookkeeping.

- Suppliers are the most likely to be flexible in their payment terms. In some cases, they will unknowingly let your account balance rise. Should you have a significant balance with a supplier that, if paid in full, would seriously damage your cash flow, consider negotiating the balance separately. In other words, if you can, freeze the old balance and pay it off over time, while opening a new account that you pay using the normal payment terms. Although this negotiation may seem one-sided in your favor, remember that the vendor would rather keep you as a customer than have you turn to a new supplier because you can't pay an old balance.

- Be careful of who you don't pay. Employee morale quickly diminishes when the paychecks are late (and in many states, fines may be imposed if complaints are filed with the Labor Relations Board). Having the phone company shut your phones down sends a very bad signal to customers. And having the landlord evict you, using rapid summary proceedings against defaulting commercial tenants, is even worse.

If your payables juggling lasts for several weeks or months, you are undercapitalized. Try to improve your cash flow or get more financing. If problems persist, see a "turnaround specialist" or a consultant specializing in distressed companies.

INVENTORY MANAGEMENT

Controlling what you buy for your business, known as *inventory management*, can free up cash for your immediate needs without the costs of obtaining additional capital. Let's say you sell socks in a clothing boutique. If you spend $25 per carton of socks, you might spend $800 to meet your annual sock inventory needs. If instead you purchase socks as needed, you leave $775 in your bank account for your current cash needs and free up storage space. This process can be repeated for every product sold at the boutique. In this case, a cash flow problem can be relieved through tighter inventory control.

Overstocking inventory has other costs as well: It increases storage costs and it invites excess shrinkage, the explained and unexplained loss of inventory. All retail operations have to deal with shrinkage. Limiting shrinkage is desirable, but in certain operations, such as restaurants, the complete elimination of shrinkage (whether due to spoilage, misportioning, or theft) is usually more costly to achieve than it is worth.

Unfortunately, predicting needed inventory levels is difficult. Changes in supplier prices or market demand can make your anticipated inventory needs incorrect. Lost sales and customer dissatisfaction can result from understocking. In order to minimize these costs, take control of your inventory management. Don't simply concern yourself with whether or not the shelves are stocked.

> **WATCHING YOUR INVENTORY**
>
> You should measure your monthly or quarterly costs of goods sold.* Take your:
> 1. Beginning inventory (BI) plus
> 2. Inventory purchases (P) during the period minus
> 3. Ending inventory (EI)
> 4. Divide that total (1. + 2. – 3.) by your sales of the inventory during the period.
>
> If that number goes up unexplainably during any period, it may signal shrinkage or inventory loss.
>
> *Mathematically: (BI + P – EI) ÷ Sales = CoGS

PRESALES

Another way to increase your available cash is to presell your goods. Let's say Joan wants to leave her job to start a software development company. She has a solid design for a computerized diet and exercise management software package. Despite the strength of the financial forecast for the project, as a single mother on a tight budget, she can't leave her job without enough cash to support her family during the development phase of the project. If she can find an interested software publisher or distributor, she may be able to presell her project. Joan would give the publisher the exclusive right to

> On obtaining capital for *Waterdance*, her award-winning, small-budget film: "The budget for the entire picture was less than my usual transportation budget, yet no one would back it because, as a producer, I was typecast. Hollywood didn't want to take a chance."
>
> –Gale Anne Hurd, producer, Terminator, Aliens, and The Abyss, speaking at a Women in Film executive luncheon in Hollywood

distribute her software once it's complete; in return, Joan would get half of the sales price up front, half upon completion, and possibly, royalties or a small share of each retail sale made in the future.

In certain industries, such as the media, advances are typical. Musicians, writers, producers, and software developers often get paid in advance for their work, usually half or more upon contract signing. In other industries, such as manufacturing and retail, presales are less common, usually limited to custom goods or special orders. Regardless, you may want to explore the possibility of prepaid sales to increase your available cash in the short term.

RETAINERS

Retainers are a type of presale used by professionals and service companies. You get paid in advance for the value of the services you agree to perform. By getting paid up front for the expected value of your services, you can have cash to cover your expenses before you do the work instead of waiting to collect at the end of the billing period.

Retainers are standard in some industries, such as the law and consulting fields. By paying a retainer, the client ensures that your time is reserved for the project and expects effective, continuous service. By requesting a retainer, you are committing yourself to a project and committing the client to (be cooperative during) the project.

Some professions have ethical guidelines preventing the recognition or use of prepaid retainers until the portion of the retainer comes due and payable. To avoid this delay, be sure to include in your retainer agreement a provision that allows you to "recognize the entire retainer into income immediately."

A *replenishable retainer* allows you to enter into a modified, continuous retainer agreement even when the expected amount of billing is unknown. Under a replenishable retainer agreement, your client refills or "replenishes" the set retainer amount each month. In effect, your client prepays each month's bill without forcing you to estimate the entire billing amount for the project in advance.

Creative Forms of Business Financing

Once you have your company operational, traditional financing techniques are not your only means of raising capital. Many a successful business has survived through entrepreneurial creativity—in their management, in their marketing, and in their financing. If the most popular and common sources of capital discussed throughout this book don't come through, all is not lost. There's still bootstrapping, bartering, and franchising to consider.

Bootstrapping

Sometimes you just have to face the facts that with no experience and only $5,000 in your savings account, you are not going to start a $50 million enterprise tomorrow. You may need to bootstrap, or start small and raise yourself up.

Take the $5,000 you have to start a fitness consulting business. You use the money to print up marketing and promotional materials so that you can attract clients. You do the consulting at the client's home to provide better

> The term *bootstrapping* comes from the idea that you have to "pull yourself up from your bootstraps." You start with nothing and build it into a productive fortune—a billion from scratch.

service (well, actually, you can't afford an office or a gym). After a few months you are building up a client base too large to service alone so you take the money you've made and hire a few employees.

Word spreads through the fitness and women's networks and your client base continues to grow. With more money coming in and more client traffic, you need an accountant and a better phone system. Your living room just won't suffice as an office any longer.

One of your clients suggests that you speak to her gym. Although the managers were not interested, you decide to ask around. Another local gym is thrilled to provide you with office space and phones as

---

ALL THE LIFE-STYLE WITHOUT ALL THE CAPITAL

Barbara Goldberg, Responsive Research, Inc., Los Angeles

Barbara Goldberg never wanted to be in the position to have a need for capital. When she started Responsive Research in 1972, she had no desire to create a large business. She had worked in the corporate world and didn't want to spend her time managing a big staff or worrying about covering high overhead expenses.

She started working out of her home and, almost twenty-five years later, she still has her office there. Her company is typically hired by Fortune 500 companies to moderate focus groups nationwide to evaluate new product ideas and advertising campaigns. Much of her work is done at night and on plane flights, working at a highly intense pace. When clients watch the focus groups behind one-way mirrors, Barbara feels like she's working in a fishbowl.

Despite the intensity, she used to find managing the slow times to be the most difficult: "When you are not picking up your paycheck every week, you need to deal with feelings of insecurity. You need to have an inherent belief in yourself that you can generate business. I know I can."

Now she uses the slow times to recharge. She has learned "to be and not do," not feeling like she constantly has to be in motion. "I take time in my Japanese garden or have a quiet lunch with my daughter."

Asked if she feels she has been successful in her venture, she confidently responds, "Yes, very much so. We all measure success in different ways. I place a high premium on my freedom and flexibility." Given her client base, track record, and many international excursions, who can disagree?

long as you refer your clients to them. The business partnership works well and the referrals flow in both directions.

The gym is ready to expand and wants you to expand with it. Although you are tempted to create a gym of your own, you realize that your core competence, the backbone of your business success, is fitness consulting. When the gym expands, you expand across the region as well. In exchange, you agree to refer your clients to the gym's nearby locations, if any.

Using a business loan to open two regional offices of your own and increase your marketing efforts, you increase your sales. To hire staff and open an office elsewhere in a neighboring state, you decide to presell discounted long-term consulting contracts. Enough clients respond to the "three year plan" to allow you to expand operations elsewhere.

With seventy employees and hundreds of clients, the capital community is suddenly interested. As far as you're concerned, it's too late. You can continue expanding slowly nationwide without sacrificing ownership to any hungry venture capitalists. At the same time you've been forced to conserve your resources and think creatively about your financing options. You have bootstrapped your dream into a national success.

Bartering

The most creative form of financing today was the primary form of doing business centuries ago—bartering. Until the creation of money, all trade was conducted by barter. You don't have to *buy* everything that you need; you can barter for some of it. Let's say you own a restaurant. Everyone needs to eat. You trade the services of a plumber for a couple of meals. You trade the services of the neon repairman for a few drinks. You offer the design consultant a free party for her daughter. And you agree to cater a family reunion for the painter.

SUBSAHARAN SILENT TRADE

Barter has been refined to an art between certain African tribespeople, but it's barter with a twist. Over the centuries, a practice has grown where the two sides never meet face to face. Instead the goods to be exchanged are placed out in the open, then the tribesmen disappear into the bush. The other side next brings its goods to the area, then slips away as well. The first side then comes back to adjust its pile and disappears again. The second group does the same. The process repeats until finally, neither side adjusts its pile. At that point, the barter is done.

The benefit of bartering is that each party is trading his or her goods or services at cost and getting the benefit of a trade at retail. For service businesses, bartering is ideal because your costs, aside from your time, are negligible. If you are a lawyer, you may be able to trade for $500 worth of services from a printer at the cost of a couple of hours to you.

Keep some cautions in mind when bartering:

- Make sure your trade is equivalent. If you earn $150 an hour, you should be getting three hours for your one with a contractor earning $50 an hour. Also remember that bartering often allows for more subjectivity in value than do cash sales, so the negotiation may not be as simple as matching your retail prices or hourly fees.
- In many cases, the trade involves projects that can become more involved than they first appear. For example, once a lawyer starts on a case, she essentially becomes professionally obliged to finish it. Avoid making bartering agreements that keep you distracted from revenue-producing projects.
- Remember your overhead. Even if you can freely trade your personal services, what about the hard costs of supplies and staff support, if any? You are also expected to pay income taxes on the value of the services you receive in trade. (Note: Although the cash economy thrives on avoiding this lesser-known provision of the tax code, you can be held legally liable for your bartered non-cash income.) Consider all your costs when bartering.

Be creative. Think of what you need and what you can trade for it. Sometimes you can even enter into a long-term barter arrangement, trading your services over time for another's. Bartering comes so naturally with our friends and family that it is often overlooked in business. As an entrepreneur, you can't afford to overlook anything.

Franchising

Most of us think of McDonalds and Kentucky Fried Chicken when we think franchise, but franchising is not limited to fast food. Franchising provides opportunity for the entrepreneur at two different stages, once at start-up and once during rapid growth.

Rather than starting your own business from scratch, you might prefer to simply be the boss at your own store. As a *franchisee*, you can purchase the right to run and control your own branch location of another's larger operation. In other words, rather than open your own deli in Topeka, you may decide to buy your own Subway

> **EE'S AND OR'S**
>
> *Franchisee :* The person or company that buys the right to open her or its own branch location of another's operation.
>
> *Franchisor :* The person or company that sells a branch location of her or its operation to another person or company.

franchise store in Topeka. As a franchisee, you get guidance throughout the entire process of opening and operating the restaurant, tremendous marketing support, and potentially, financing assistance.

On the other hand, if you already have a successful business and are looking to expand to other locations, becoming a *franchisor* may be the right move for you. As a franchisor, you get expansion capital from the managers of your new location. Although you lose direct ownership of the new store, you can arrange to take a share of the profits, retain the right to ensure quality control, and at the same time, increase the value of your company.

BECOMING A FRANCHISEE

Not every entrepreneur starts from the ground up. Some purchase existing businesses and don't change a thing. Others buy a franchise.

Being a franchisee has its pros and cons. Interestingly enough, it is the same list—it depends on your perspective. Among the advantages/disadvantages of being a franchisee are:

- You are buying a proven concept. (You don't get to create and test your own concept.)
- Market studies have been performed to determine the optimal franchise store locations. (You don't have complete autonomy in selecting your retail space or negotiating the terms of your lease.)
- You have help starting up operations. (You are told how to operate.)
- You are given management training and operational guides. (You do not have complete autonomy in designing operations, menus, product inventory, etc.)
- You are given marketing and promotional materials and there are regional or national advertisements for your franchise. (Someone else controls your marketing and market strategy.)

Since 1989, firms have specifically been targeting women as franchisees. Originally, women were considered inappropriate candidates for most franchises, including fast food and printing, but women have since proven themselves as franchisees.

Source: Barbara Marsh, "More Firms Target Women as Prospective Franchisees," Wall Street Journal, 1989.

In some cases, the franchisor is more interested in recruiting dedicated, capable management to own and run the franchise than the franchisor is in raising capital. These franchisors are often willing to help you with financing. The process is similar to seller financing. The franchisor may be willing to lower the sale price in return for a (larger) share of the profits from the store, or offer you a loan or line of credit directly.

Although franchisors are typically responsible for site selection, many franchisors will accept the unsolicited requests of potential franchisees. To learn more about franchise opportunities in your area, watch the "business to business" section of your local newspaper's classified ads. If you want to open a particular franchise store in your location, you can contact that company directly.

BECOMING A FRANCHISOR

If you build a business where the name and operation of the company can carry the business forward, even in the absence of specific individuals, you may have the beginnings of a franchise.

A franchisable concept has these characteristics:

- Success in one location can be replicated elsewhere.
- Intensive training or centralized management is not required.
- The company name has a loyal customer base that contributes to its success at each location.
- An individual branch location of the company can benefit from the centralized purchasing of supplies.
- An individual branch location of the company can benefit from regional or national advertising.

You will probably want to consider franchising out your operation only if you are in the restaurant or retail industry. Service companies usually have a harder time operating without the members of their organization. Most service businesses prefer a centralized management system where the company's headquarters oversee operations to ensure quality control. When you franchise, someone else owns the branch location and has the right to hire her own staff.

Manufacturers and wholesalers normally would not benefit from franchising either. They usually profit from economies of scale—increased production and distribution translates into lower costs per unit and higher profits. Producers also might find it easier to license their products to other companies rather than to franchise. You would typically franchise the value of your company name and concept; you would license your products and inventions.

As a *franchisor*, you gain capital by essentially selling the right to use your company name. As additional incentive you provide advertising, promotional items, operational handbooks, and training. The *franchisee* pays you according to a payment schedule to get and keep the franchise. In many cases, the franchisor will keep "company stores" in addition to the franchises sold to franchisees. In other words, you own some of the stores yourself and you sell other stores to franchisees.

The timing and amount of payment varies tremendously. Typically, the franchisee pays a down payment and monthly or annual fees. The fees could be fixed, a percentage of sales, or both. Some franchisors don't even charge a fee but instead require that their supplies and distributors be used

FRANCHISE BENEFITS

Franchising is not only used to raise more capital. Some entrepreneurs find selling franchises as the best way to attract good management. No managers are more responsible than the owners themselves. These franchisors concerned with recruiting management often require that the franchise owners work full time at their stores.

exclusively. Other franchisors charge a larger, one-time fee to purchase a franchise.

Money, Money Everywhere

When you get right down to it, venture capitalists do not have a hold on the investment marketplace. Sources of capital are everywhere. Aside from friends, family, private investors, federal and state government funds, business sellers, and corporate partners, consider:

- vendors
- customers
- landlords

Your suppliers may be happy to extend trade credit, which gives you a longer period of time before you have to pay for supplies. In the interim, you can sell the supplies you receive (in the form of your product) and use those revenues to pay the bill. This approach is especially useful for growing companies when the increase in sales comes after the increase in supplies needed.

Customers are also a viable source of capital. In some cases, selling memberships, subscriptions, or discounted advance purchases of a service or product can provide the funds. In others, large buyers may be willing to finance the start-up of your operation in return for exclusive contracting rights or special service. One minority entrepreneur was financed by a regional telephone company to get the business started. The utility company then used the small business, which supplied specialized equipment to the telephone company, to meet its Section 8(a) minority contracting goals.

The landlord is another potential source of capital. For many businesses, rent is the single largest expense next to payroll. To minimize the expense, many entrepreneurs have successfully negotiated with their landlords prior to setting foot in the rented space. The landlord may be willing to forgo some rent in the beginning of the operation to fill the space. Or the landlord may agree to provide your leasehold improvements or changes you want to make in the property now in return for repayment with interest or equity in the future. In one case, the landlord offered free office space to an entrepreneurial professional if the consultant would periodically do work for the landlord and his tenants.

Percentage of sales leases are possible when the landlord accepts rent in the form of a set percentage of your sales. Another common lease involves the landlord accepting a lower base amount of rent in return for a share of the revenues above a certain amount each month. In other words, the landlord is willing to risk taking less in rent now, especially from retail operations, for a larger share of your profits later.

Regardless of how you finance the growth of your business once it's operational, the jewel of all capital sources awaits for those businesses that thrive—Wall Street. Reaching public sources of capital, whether obtained through a public or private offering, involves significant legal formalities. Should your concept be strong enough or your venture be successful enough, you can move from business sources of capital to the potentially more lucrative public sources.

Resources and References

Bruce Blechman's and Jay Conrad Levinson's *Guerrilla Financing* (Boston: Houghton Mifflin, 1991) is an excellent resource for creatively using your assets, whether personal or business, to get capital. The book focuses on nontraditional methods of obtaining financing.

To find business financing companies, first contact your local bank. Even if they don't do factoring and inventory or equipment financing, they may help you locate other local financing institutions that do. Also be sure to check your yellow pages for factoring, financing, and leasing companies.

For more information on the asset valuation process as well as other analytical techniques used by bankers and accountants, read Erich A. Helfert's classic *Techniques of Financial Analysis* (Boston: Irwin, 1991).

CHAPTER 7

Networking with Purpose

Most of us experience moments of fear putting ourselves forward in certain social settings. Even the most aggressive entrepreneur can falter when faced with a roomful of people she doesn't know.

Learning the art of networking provides you an entry into any circle you wish to know. Networking has become so pervasive that international management consultant Peter Drucker now calls us "the network society." Let's start with some simple rules of the game. Some are as fresh as today's latest technology, but most of them derive from the rules of simple etiquette. If nothing else, respecting others, listening sincerely, speaking openly, appreciating another's time, and behaving with courtesy will ensure that you network well.

> "The cardinal principle of etiquette is thoughtfulness."
>
> —Emily Post

Emily Card's Networking Rules

Properly handling a networking event can be an intimidating task. The following rules will help you to network with effect.

1. "Advance" your events. Political advance people know how to get a candidate gracefully in and out of several events scheduled for the same time slot. You can do the same for yourself by stacking events in an evening. Scheduling for maximum effect involves delicately inquiring about the peak moment of the party without being rude. The best approach: "Unfortunately, I have a prior conflicting engagement, but I really want to hear the guest speaker. What time are you planning the remarks?" Or ask: "When is dinner being served?"

2. Never directly ask, "Who's coming?"   It's rude to appear interested in attending an event only if others of interest will be there. The host (and committee, if there is one) have honored you by extending an invitation. It's your job to scope out the situation without directly confronting the guest list. You might properly say, "I have so looked forward to meeting Ms. Curdle, who I understand is a member. Do you know whether she'll be coming?" A savvy person on the other end may then highlight some of the key people planning to come. Another approach: "I'm new to the organization. Can you tell me the key people I should be sure to meet?"

3. Practice your "sound bite."   Be able to describe yourself and your mission in a memorable sentence or two. If your conversation is interrupted, the groundwork is laid for a future phone call or reception.

4. If possible, take someone with you to the event, even if only for moral support.   Selling yourself is one of the most difficult tasks on earth. A supporter, an aide, or a friend can make us feel more secure when we go where we are strangers. Politicians can teach us here as well. You may have noticed that only the exceptional politician travels alone. Having someone to help you remember who you met and to keep you grounded in your goals at hand can be a great help, as well as taking the edge off the experience of entering a room alone.

5. Before you head toward a meeting, be completely ready.   Stop by the ladies' room, check that you feel exactly the way you want about yourself. Take a few extra breaths.

Once I was with a very well-known woman about to join a crowded reception in her honor. I was nervous because I was eager to get her into the room. At first I waited impatiently, then fascinated as I watched her do more than straighten her hair. In front of the mirror, I saw her public persona slip into place as she centered herself and then stood quietly, absolutely still, before turning to sail out of the door full of confidence. I always think of this moment whenever I am rushing to a meeting, and I try to treat myself as if I, too, deserve this moment's pause. You deserve it as well. Take it.

6. Enter a room purposefully.   In older editions of Emily Post's *Etiquette*, the manner of entering a drawing room was described. Even though nobody calls them "drawing rooms" today, Emily Post's rules still hold. "There should be no more difficulty in entering the drawing-room of Mrs. Worldly than in entering the sitting-room at home . . . . The way not to enter a drawing-room is to dart forward and then

stand awkwardly bewildered and looking about in every direction."
(Emily Post, *Etiquette*, 10th Ed., New York: Harper & Row, p. 86.)

When entering a doorway to a reception or other business or
social gathering, pause long enough to give yourself time to get
oriented.

7. Find your host first.   As you pause at the door, look for your
host. If at all possible, head directly to her to say hello before you get
caught up in the party. If the host is not immediately evident or otherwise engaged, then spot another person that you know or would
like to meet.

8. Seek out the guest of honor.   Introduce yourself. If the guest of
honor is to speak, don't quiz him about the topic of the talk—most
speakers want to keep their thoughts fresh for their audiences. By
saying hello before the speech, you allow yourself a private moment
that will be hard to get afterward, when most people feel less shy
about approaching the speaker. Afterward, even with a crowd
around, you can still go up, nod briefly, and thank the speaker.

9. Use the beginning of the party.   All of us are nervous at the
beginning of an event. From hostess anxiety to guest-of-honor jitters,
there are a few magic minutes before the party "jells." If you are new
too, come at the stated hour and take that opportunity to reach out
before the key people become distracted with the sheer volume of
interactions.

10. Work the room.   Take another tip from the politicians. No good
politician leaves an event without shaking as many hands as possible.
Especially if you are new to an organization, a business arena, or a
geographic area, use this technique to see people you want to work
with later.

11. Put others at ease by being at ease yourself.   No matter how shy
you are, someone out there is shyer. If you need a boost, seek out a
quiet person and get to know her. You'll be pleasantly surprised.

12. Listen with attention.   Sometimes in an effort to meet as many
people as possible at a gathering, we find ourselves craning our necks
to look for our next contact. Everyone is guilty at some time or
another of this sin. Try to keep your mind on the person with whom
you are talking. If you are looking for someone in particular, say so
right at the beginning: "Won't you help me keep my eye out for Jane
Smith? I promised myself I would say hello today."

Powerful people often learn the trick of concentrating absolutely on whomever they are speaking with. Try to cultivate this talent.

13. *Notice repeat contacts.* If you find people at several different kinds of meetings, you've found skilled networkers. Usually, these people are opinion leaders as well, because they move in many circles and know leaders in each. Anthropologists doing field work look for these people to become "informants," people versed in a culture who can guide the way to its mores. You can do the same, calling on the people who seem to be in most demand for your own peek into the culture of the organization or business.

14. *Recognize that everyone is a buyer* and *seller.* Don't be nervous about the fact that you are selling something too. For example, you may be selling your business to find capital, but you are also buying an investor. Even though you might be "needy" now, if you are successful, the very person you are trying to impress will need you in the future. Don't forget your own value, even if it's all potential.

15. *Understand that saying so makes it so.* If your plan is to open a company that manufactures record boxes, don't say, "I'm sort of thinking of, well, I don't know for sure, but I think I might start a company." Say instead: "I own a company that manufactures record boxes." Or, "My company is in the finishing stages of developing a new record box."

A talented screenwriter started as a homemaker. At her first writing seminar, the instructor encouraged the students to have cards and stationery printed with the title "screenwriter" under their names. Before writing the first scene, Janie was out ordering her stationery. When her first script was finished, she had the paper ready to send it out. At industry events in the meanwhile, her card introduced where she was going—"screenwriter"—not where she was coming from—"housewife."

16. *Exchange cards.* The exchange of cards has become so commonplace that women who work in the home find themselves pulling check deposit stubs out and tearing off their names and addresses at cocktail parties. Or better yet, printing their own cards. Whatever your stage of business, be prepared with plenty of cards at any function you attend, however seemingly "social." I find it a great help to put a stack of cards in my pocket, if I have one, or in an accessible open side pocket of my purse so that I can pull them straight out without having to fumble with cards, drinks, handshakes, and purses all at once.

17. Mixers are for getting acquainted, not for long personal or philosophical discussions.   Save the complex stuff for later. Use a networking occasion to touch bases and move on.

Most people at mixers want to do just that. Save getting to know a person well for a later, more private setting. Even if you click with someone, remember her and return later in the evening rather than monopolize her time. This rule holds especially true for the guest of honor, speakers, hosts, or celebrities of any stripe.

18. Networking is for meeting, not eating.   Take a tip from Scarlett O'Hara and eat before the event if you're there for serious networking. You'll pass up great caviar, fabulous smoked salmon, and delicious hot hors d'oeuvres, but you'll gain the ability to concentrate 100 percent on the people around you, not to mention not worrying about food caught in your teeth. If you are too busy to eat before the event, go straight to the table, eat, freshen up, and then begin networking.

If you're presenting yourself at a serious business party, you should also omit or limit your drinks. Usually bottled water or a soda presents a better choice and a better image. Best: Have something to quench your thirst and then leave your hands free to greet others and make notes on their cards, if appropriate, for follow-up.

19. Treat the staff politely.   My mother always said, "You can tell a lady by how she treats the servants." The modern equivalent means showing respect for the staff of an event (or for that matter, for anyone with whom you are dealing). Using the golden rule works wonders when you need special favors later, whether it's the name and address of someone you met or an invitation to the next event. Or, as the *Los Angeles Times* reported, "You know you're in Hollywood when" at a recent reception for a studio screening, a studio exec and an agent were discussing a script. The bartender leaned over and said, "Yes, I've read it, it's a great script."

Don't forget the staff is also a pipeline to the top. If my secretary, Roz, screened someone out because she hadn't shown her basic business courtesy, Roz's decision usually stood. Many executives feel this way too—busy people don't want to deal with those who don't take time to be polite to others around them.

20. Always ask key people for others they recommend you meet.
Take seriously any such suggestion, but don't ask them to introduce you. If you're at an event, you might say, "I've never met Joe Dugan, would it be possible for you to point him out?" The polite response is to offer you an introduction. But sometimes other variables make that

offer uncomfortable, especially if you have just met the person of whom you're asking the favor and Joe Dugan is a powerful figure in the potential introducer's life. Remember, introduction, formally speaking, represents a kind of vouching for someone else. Don't push this one.

21. *Always take time to thank the host.* Never leave without thanking the host unless you're departing early and a thank you would be disruptive to the program.

22. *Immediately put all the cards from the event into an envelope marked with the date and name of the event.* Before you go to sleep that night, or the next morning before you begin your day, take time to put the cards you've collected in a separate envelope with date and event. Note key points on the card right while you are with the person or as soon as you can afterward. Far from appearing weird, people respect the fact that you take them and yourself seriously enough to make a note of any agreed-on follow-up.

If it would be awkward to jot down notes in someone's face (for example, you're trying to be low key or you have thought of a connection you haven't yet discussed with the particular individual), take a moment when you powder your nose to pull the card out and put a key word to remind you later. When I was in Africa doing field research, people were skittish about having their interviews written down. I developed the technique of leaving an interview and immediately writing down all that had transpired before I moved on to the next location. Today, when I feel that the next train of events may erase the immediate energy and information from this one, I may pull my car over and make a few notes before entering a room with a new set of people. Or, if time doesn't permit, before I go to bed I try to stack the cards by event and make any special notations. It may take months to get back to those notes, but I can always locate the person I met in a distant city by finding her envelope in the red folder I have reserved for recent events. You may also find that adding names to a computerized database helps as well—I do that too as time permits—but I find that a visual reminder of the person, in the form of her card, helps jog my memory the best.

23. *Send notes to the key people you met.* Send a thank-you note to the host remarking on your host's graciousness or on the speaker's contribution to your understanding of an issue. It's the polite thing to do as well as an effective tool for later opening doors.

If you possibly can, jot an informal note or type a more formal one to people with whom you hope to connect later. Include a piece of publicity about yourself or your business, if appropriate, or re-enclose your business card.

24. Follow up with people in demand; they will expect you to.   After a day or two has passed, if you have found someone important to your mission, follow up with a telephone call. If that person's schedule is such that they are hard to reach on the telephone, then ask the assistant about a good time to call back or whether you could schedule a telephone appointment.

25. If possible, take someone to tea or coffee.   The person who requests a follow-up meeting is expected to be the host. If you would like an informal session and your budget limits the lunches you can host, ask a person whether he could take time out for a cup of coffee at a location near his office. Even if he says no, the likelihood is that you'll receive an invitation to drop by his office for a chat—much better than inviting yourself for a follow-up meeting.

NETWORKING SUPPLIES

Before you run out to network, make sure you have the following networking supplies ready:

✔ Up-to-date calling or *business cards*. Don't tear off checkbook deposit slips. If you are a homemaker, just have a simple card with your name, address, and telephone. The minute you change addresses or telephone numbers, get new cards, even if they are temporary and not your up-to-the minute design. Otherwise, the chief impression you'll leave is one of instability.

✔ Plenty of plain business *envelopes* for the cards you collect.

✔ A distinctive *folder* to keep the cards so you can find them later.

✔ A *database* of some kind, whether automated on your computer, a typed list of contacts, a Rolodex, or a plastic card box.

✔ *Informal note cards* with your name or initials on the front. If necessary, get preprinted informals at the stationery store with your first initial.

✔ More *formal note cards* if you can afford them. Many executives prefer a card with their name engraved at the top. Matching envelopes with your address on the back flap complete this ensemble.

✔ Try to have your cards *match your informals* so that if you include your card, the recipient receives a small, coordinated package from you.

✔ A working *answering machine* or voice mail.

✔ A *fax and dedicated fax number*.

✔ A *business mailing address*, if you don't have an office, where you can collect your mail and receive deliveries.

IF YOU ONLY HAVE TIME TO DO ONE THING, PUT THE CARDS OF THE PEOPLE YOU MEET IN AN ENVELOPE MARKED WITH THE DATE AND NAME OF THE EVENT. Like any other entrepreneur, sometimes I get super busy and my follow-up slides. But I can always find the envelope which keeps the cards in the context of the event and reconnect later.

The Four Stages of Networking
The authors of a helpful networking book, *52 Ways to Re-Connect, Follow Up, & Stay in Touch...When You Don't Have Time to Network* (Anne Baber and Lynne Waymon, Dubuque, IA: Kendall/Hunt Publishing Company, 1994) suggest that networking goes in stages: taking, trading, teaching, and trusting.

During the *taking* stage, people tend to focus on themselves and their needs. "But, the best networkers approach the process with the opposite point of view. They give more than they get."

Trading involves exchanging something of value. With just trades, people produce the "single sale" rather than developing relationships.

The *teaching* stage involves both teaching other people what you need and learning what they need. The authors suggest that it's not whom you know or what you know, but *who knows you*. "You don't have a networking relationship until your contact knows you so well that, when an opportunity comes by that you would benefit from, your contact calls or writes you." This sort of networking involves building a consistent image or message about yourself and your work, one that is easy to grasp and remember because it has a "hook." In journalism, the hook is the lead to a story, the sentence or angle that that catches the reader's attention up front. The whole story hangs on the hook.

The final stage of networking is *trusting*. When you get to networking relationships based on trust, they pay off. Networking is not only about gathering cards or looking for your needs. You want to develop lasting, long-term relationships as well. When you have trusting relationships, you can count on others to help you as they can count on you.

To network to raise capital, you have to use all four of these stages, depending upon your own growth level as a networker. The neophyte businessperson who has a lightbulb idea but not much more in terms of a business plan, an advisory board, or community contacts, will have to begin the process of networking just to identify the players.

> "People change and forget to tell each other."
> —Lillian Hellman

At the opposite extreme is the "plugged in" person who seemingly knows everyone. Depending on how that person has presented herself in the past, her challenge may lie in gaining credibility as anentrepreneur capable of succeeding in her new venture. Sometimes switching images is as hard to do as creating them; not everyone is comfortable with multifaceted individuals capable of conquering many worlds.

Remember What You're Networking For—Money

General networking is great. You can improve your social life, making many acquaintances who turn into friends. You can become an active member of your community, and even raise money for worthy causes. You can learn new skills that enhance your business. You can expand your customer base or your advisory board. You may meet your banker, your next CFO, or a new supplier. While all these networking moments have their own raison d'être, *your purpose here is to complete the circle necessary to raise business capital.* Keep your eye on the ball. The ball should have dollar signs on it when you are networking for capital.

The name of the game isn't opportunism. You mustn't feel that just because you need money you are using the people you meet. Your objective now as an entrepreneur happens to be raising capital. Other people have different objectives. Remember, we are all buyers and sellers.

Right now you are a seller—of your business potential. Your investment will make money for the buyers. It may give them a chance to engage in socially responsible investing. They may also be helping the economic bottom line of the country. Remember the flow of capital. Money left lying in savings banks doesn't create jobs; money put to work through entrepreneurs builds the economic fabric of our society.

The extent to which we are all both buyers and sellers is constantly illustrated by networking follow-up letters, such as the one quoted at the side. This entrepreneur both saw investment opportunities for herself and simultaneously wanted to explore locating expansion capital.

Fund-raisers recognize that even if the event committee could donate the entire amount raised in an evening, hosting a shared activity produces broader support. Likewise, your networking to raise capital produces more than money. It produces a shared sense of undertaking, a shared sense of responsibility in the community, a base of supporters, and a network that can produce more support, more investors, and more personal connections.

> **SAMPLE FOLLOW-UP LETTER**
>
> "Thank you for including me in the exciting evening last Friday. I met many friends and clients, along with some very interesting new people. Do keep me posted on available investment opportunities.
>
> "On another note entirely, I have realized over the years that with an infusion of capital, I could expand my company to four or five more locations around the country. Now more than ever before I feel my concept could be marketed nationally."

Where to Network

While groups can be divided and subdivided into many types, for capital accumulation purposes, your focus has to be on groups that do one of the following:

(a) contain the people with money that you seek
(b) consciously and purposefully seek investors
(c) provide leads to get back to the "a" groups

> "Networking organizations are important, but there is a limit to what you can do as an individual. Choose somewhere that provides opportunities for your business. I don't know how to tell you to make that choice. You have homework to do."
>
> —*Doris Thomas, past president, Dallas–Fort Worth NAWBO chapter*

To find people with money to invest, you have to be where people with money congregate. Either you meet them as peers in country clubs, exclusive city clubs, expensive health spas and hotels, or in their community organizations, such as churches, synagogues, or industry associations. Or you meet them as "customers" of their causes—charitable and political fund-raisers. By paying a ticket price and picking the right events, you can meet the elite on their own grounds and they will be glad to have you there.

The best place to start is with people you know and branch out from there. Networking among your own friends and family statistically provides the best chance of capital success. From there, individual investors are the ticket to start-up.

Individual Investors

The individuals you seek may not be known to you personally, but the best way to meet someone you have identified as a potential supporter is to look for others who may know the person or at least have an acquaintance with her. While meeting a Rockefeller might be a tall order, most of us can find someone who knows someone who knows someone. The concept of "six degrees of separation" expresses the notion that all of us can get to anyone if we go through six intervening people. While nine, fifteen, or thirty-three degrees might be more like it, through a bit of digging you can find the connections you seek.

If you truly have no idea where to start, look the person up at your local library in one of the computerized periodical indexes. Scan as many articles as it takes to locate some connection you can access, however remote. You may have gone to the same university. She may be a member of an organization that your uncle also joined. Perhaps she lives near a friend, goes to temple nearby, or is appearing locally to make a speech. Follow the leads, however slim, until you reach the potential investor.

An opposite approach that may work better is to start with lists of people you do know. See how many of them are potential investors or may know potential investors. Rather than create an ideal list of people who may be impossible to interest, develop a list of practical connections you can make.

The best plan: Combine the two approaches and come up with a targeted list of five, ten, or a hundred people that you need to meet to take your next steps.

JOAN'S ONE HUNDRED

Joan was starting an advertising company. While she knew many people in the highly competitive industry on the West coast, she didn't know Madison Avenue types. She made a list of one hundred people that she wanted to meet. When she attended trade shows and industry events, she made a point of meeting these people. Within a year, Joan had met all one hundred.

The adage "be careful what you ask for" comes to mind. It seemed that by simply listing these people, Joan had already created the energy and attitude necessary for the circumstances to arise. Now Joan's company has been acquired by a top advertising firm—headed by one of her original "one hundred."

If you have a few dollars to invest in meeting people with money, the quickest way to find and meet them is at fund-raisers open to anyone who can muster the price of a ticket.

FUND-RAISERS

If you read the social or life-style pages of your local paper, you'll see that people with money spend much of their social lives at fund-raising events. If you know of an individual or group of individuals with whom you would like to come into contact, get in touch with the organizers of the event and offer to volunteer in exchange for a free ticket. Or, if the ticket is within your budget—and some great events go cheap, depending on the city and the season—then buy a ticket and make the rounds.

Your goal here: Exchange cards with as many people as you can. Do not try to pitch your business. It's impolite at a social setting and won't gain your objective, which is to get to know the people you're interested in connecting with for investment. Instead, work the room and talk about things that you have in common, including the event that you are attending. Suggest lunch or tea later or say you'll give George Oldfamily a call. Leave it at that. Follow up with an informal "Nice to meet you at the pinecone fund-raiser. I especially enjoyed

---

WHERE TO NETWORK

Women's business groups
General business groups
The Chamber of Commerce
Social groups
Community groups
The PTA
Churches and temples
Spas
Country clubs
Junior League
Alumni associations
Fund-raisers

your comments on acorns." (If you don't have "informals" or notes with your name on them, now's the time to order some conservative ones. They are perfect for these follow-ups and save you a world of time, plus they provide a personal touch.)

Later, follow up more formally, with a meeting if you can. If not, send along your business plan or the executive summary.

Venture Capitalists

Your challenge, should you decide to enter the VC market for money, will be to find venture capitalists who both understand your business and are willing to invest in it.

The world of venture capital, as a small, tight-knit world, is very much built on who you know. Networking skills can make a big difference as you approach that marketplace. Not only should you get to know key VCs, but you'll also want to be acquainted with other groups in your region or industry. If you identify yourself as a lawyer, you're expected to know other lawyers. If you identify yourself with a local community, you're expected to have contacts in that community. Or if you are a female high-tech player breaking into the new media industry, even if you don't ordinarily network with women, you'd better make the acquaintance of distribution consultant Joey Tamer because, like it or not, you'll be assumed to know other important peers (read *women*) in your field.

When meeting a VC, you want to come on strong, secure, and centered. Word gets around fast about half-baked ideas and half-formed schemes. Your idea can be different—after all, it is the creation of new industries that generates the highest returns (Federal Express)—but your business plans have to be completely thought out.

Women's Venture Groups

Within government, strides have been taken to create an environment directly supportive of investing in women. The efforts in the private sector haven't caught up. Historically, the various venture capital communities formed around SBA efforts. The National Association of Investment Companies (NAIC) grew out of the MESBICs, minority enterprise small business investment companies. No similar organization exists for women because until very recently, women were not defined as minorities for the purpose of government SBIC assistance.

While many businesses are women-owned or women-led, the first serious national effort to put capital into women's hands has just begun. The formation of the Capital Circle suggests a model for the future, a national group of prominent investors and women with economic policy clout, banded together with the mission of mobilizing capital for women-led businesses.

There are also several funds being created that target women-led ventures as investments. Early entries include Chicago-based Inroads Capital Partners, Philadelphia-based Women's Collateral Funding, Boulder's Women's Equity Fund, and Blue Chip Capital of Cincinnati.

Selling Yourself

When you are networking, you're not just selling a concept or your business. You are selling something tangible; you are selling yourself.

Business plans may loom large in the judgment of professional advisors, whether lawyers, bankers, or accountants. It's their job, in particular, to make sure you have taken care of the myriad of legal and accounting details that add up to the necessary formal underpinnings. Legal requirements must be met. For the investor's advisors, the business plan and accompanying documents should be letter-perfect. For the investor, you, the entrepreneur, need not be.

You need to be yourself and present that self to your advantage. After all, when you're on your own, if your natural instincts don't guide you to business success, your investor shouldn't consider you.

Where dedication to the job is at issue, women (and single-parent men, older entrepreneurs, minority entrepreneurs—anyone who doesn't fit the twenty-five-year-old, hot-shot, techno-macho male model) need to find creative solutions to the "breakfast problem." Invite your prospect to join you and the kids for breakfast and then accompany you through your day. Be careful here—an attorney who took her ten-year-old for a coffee meeting with a colleague was surprised to find the colleague rattled by the experience. If your children are not very well behaved, forget that idea and consider tea instead. Get a sitter and stay late—ask for a nine P.M. meeting due to the "press of business."

> "If a business person won't meet you at seven A.M., think twice about their commitment to long hours."
>
> —Chuck Brose, TMR Corporation, a venture capitalist

The point is to demonstrate commitment and dedication without falling into the trap of requiring yourself to engage in behaviors that you cannot sustain as an entrepreneur. Of course, to get the money you may have to go to great lengths. An enterprising television producer who couldn't get a meeting with the network executive flew to France and "ran into her" at a trade show. The sale was concluded in the more relaxed and open environment where the executive's job at hand was to sell, rather than buy, so her "no's" weren't in place.

> "'Nine to five'—that's a dream a working mother never experiences. Any woman who can work a full-time job and raise a family can run a business, if that's her choice."
>
> —Anne Watts

The "Vision Thang"

Investors look for vision. An entrepreneur without vision, however local in scope the venture, is an entrepreneur ill-prepared for rainy days.

An entrepreneur, like a president, needs an agenda. Themes won't do. Themes are soft, theoretical, and idiosyncratic; agendas are hard, action-oriented, and directed. Agendas should be consistently presented in your networking and your business plan to guide the investor to your vision and goals. While you wouldn't want to scare your prospective investor by your fervent belief that with your new bottle top you'll become the richest woman in the world, you'd certainly want to share the breadth and scope of your thinking if it extends that far.

> "Don't be afraid of the space between your dreams and reality. If you can dream it, you can make it so."
>
> —Belva Davis

If you have trouble with the vision thing, then take time to get in touch with your own creative center. Give your ideas a chance to incubate. Sometimes we are so caught up in the day-to-day process of keeping our computers going, our payrolls met, and our clothes pressed that we forget to return to and *communicate* our vision. Almost without exception, investors want entrepreneurs who have some spark that distinguishes them from the herd. Use your vision to sell yourself. If you believe in it, it's the one sales tool that won't fail you.

Getting the Cash

Ultimately, to get money, you have to ask for it. Very few people hand over checks without being asked. If you find someone who does, call us.

> **GIVING IT AWAY**
>
> $124.31 billion was donated in charitable contributions in 1992 compared to $2.5 billion invested by the venture capital industry in the same year.
>
> Source: American Association of Fund-Raising Counsel Trust for Philanthropy and the Small Business Administration.

People with money take money seriously, and they don't part with it easily. It's an axiom among fundraisers that it's easier to get people to give away $10,000 than to invest $1,000. Why the contrast? Because the two actions involve different impulses, both with a heavy emotional component. Giving to charity or political candidates puts resources on the line with intangible, indirect returns. Investing involves tangible, measurable returns (or losses). No one likes to lose money or play the sucker; most everyone wants to help others. But investing isn't charity, even when the investors are motivated, in part, by social goals.

Fund-raisers also know that one of the worst mistakes you can make is failing to "qualify your donor" by determining the investor's capacity prior to solicitation. Make sure that the amount you ask for matches the capacity, with a little stretch included for good measure. The potential $5,000 donor to arthritis research who responds to a $50 pledge card now feels she has fulfilled her obligation. The big-money donor must be qualified and approached by telephone or in person, while the $50 donor is often content with a postal solicitation. Conversely, if you ask the $50 donor for $5,000, she'll be equally turned off, feeling that her $50 would be meaningless if $5,000 is needed.

These observations lead to the following guidelines on asking for investment money:

1. Qualify your investor.
2. Ask in person or by telephone.
3. Wait until the time is right, but don't wait too long.
4. Take no for an answer—but not the first time you hear it. Try to turn the first no into a maybe and find a way to leave the door open.
5. Ask seriously.
6. If you receive a check in person, put it in an envelope rather than throw it into your pocketbook or briefcase. This behavior indicates your sense of responsibility for the funds.
7. Ask a hundred people for every investor you hope to get.
8. Make certain the investor understands what percentage of the total investment is involved.
9. Take your investment in stages. Get a promise for more and take less initially. Taking the money in increments shows your respect for the investor's opportunity cost and your acknowledgment that if your business doesn't go according to plan, the investor shouldn't invest more.
10. Set investment goals the way that universities set contribution targets—so many at $100,000, so many at $50,000, so many at $1,000. Industry norms may dictate "units" of specific sizes, but even investment units can be broken down into smaller chunks.
11. Don't worry about "using up your chips." Stale chips are worthless.
12. Use your lead investors to open doors and keep them open. Once you get a single investor committed, that person has a stake in your success. Use that involvement to get other investors committed.

It's the Gut, Stupid

When all is said and done, investors first and foremost use their instincts when making their decisions. If your business doesn't match an investor's instincts, there's little you can do after you've done the obvious. Time to pick up your business plan and your smile and move on.

Eventually, you'll find investors that fit. And the ones that passed today may rethink their reactions when success comes knocking at your door.

Networking with Women: Does It Make a Difference?

Men may have controlled business and capital for thousands of years through informal mechanisms, but when it comes to formal networking, women today have the edge. Feeling the need to play catch-up, women looked around in the early 1970s and realized that to compete in a world that required women to work twice as hard and be three times as good, women had to organize. Like immigrants to new cities in the Third World, who band together in voluntary associations to provide moral and financial support to one another, women started one after another group called "women in. . . ." Women in Business, Women in Film, Women in Communications, Women in Advertising, Women in Political Science, and Women in African Studies, to name a few, became a point of connection for the few women in each field nationally.

> Gloria Steinem has pointed out that women in the workplace are like immigrant groups within this country. Like these groups, she says, women will need to employ the tactics that have made them so successful.
>
> —*Gloria Steinem, in* Interview, *June 1995*

Queen bees of yesteryear were out; organized interaction with other women around a mission was in. The result: a stunning national system of women's networks, so effective that women now network networks. This networking holds the greatest promise for quickly eliminating the capital gap.

> "You can use networking skills to find creative solutions to your business challenges, but money follows money, investors follow success, and business is business."
>
> —*Anonymous woman who believes single-gender networking is not the route to business success*

Some women continue to resist networking with other women, insisting that they want to work in a gender-neutral world and simply don't have time to spend in any organizational endeavor, no matter how worthy. Increasingly, however, women have found that because of the late entry of women into the business world, the lack of mentors, and the particular concerns of women in business, women should network with women. Associations for women business owners, budding female entrepreneurs, women of particular ethnic backgrounds, women in particular industries, and women

> "The old boys' network is dead, but women haven't realized it yet."
>
> —*Business school graduate*

interested in general networking have taken center stage in many business-women's lives.

Is the Old Boys' Network Dead?

Observing the ferocity with which women of a certain age network, many young men and some young women are unsure of the need. In many respects, the old boys' network is dead, or at least dying with the last survivors.

Many male college graduates repeat the same observation, "My friends don't network. My generation certainly doesn't network by gender. We went to school with men and women, became friends with men and women, and stay connected with men and women."

Although the older generation of men still enjoy their exclusive privileges, over time, as the younger generation pervades the workforce, more egalitarian models will prevail. Of course, change is coming slowly on this front. Women still comprise a significant minority of the business school populations today, but today young men are as aware of the imbalance as their female colleagues.

Whether and to what extent mainstream men are networking remains subject to interpretation. It seems that men today tend to network locally, either in a specific region, a specific industry, or both. Men also may rely on existing informal networks of friends and acquaintances rather than take the more proactive networking approach that has become popular with women.

By contrast, for many women an "old girls' network" has been born that enables a new way of business

"Old boys' networks" were a natural outgrowth of old school ties built at exclusively male private schools. The term goes back to exclusive British "public"—as distinct from home tutoring—private schools that educated the elite. Once male-only U.S. topflight private schools and Ivy League colleges created the same sort of old school ties, groupings that naturally form networks of business and social ties. People tend to do business within these networks.

WOMEN'S ADVOCACY ORGANIZATIONS

	NUMBER
National Association of Women's Business Yellow Pages	1,000,000
National Association of Female Executives	250,000
Soroptomist International of the Americas	95,000
American Business Women's Association	90,000
National Federation of Women's Business and Professional Clubs	80,000
Zonta International	36,000
American Women's Economic Development Corporation	8,000
Coalition of 100 Black Women	7,000
National Association of Women Business Owners	5,000
International Alliance	5,000
National Association of Black Women Entrepreneurs	5,000
National Federation of Black Women Business Owners	3,200
International Women's Forum	2,750
Women in Film	2,500

life. Some women do so much business with other women they are hard-pressed to conform to expected norms when suddenly thrust into a predominantly male group. Reams of material have been produced to highlight the stylistic and actual differences of women's business behavior. For some women, the more comfortable path has been to work exclusively with other women rather than having to tend to the constant communication challenges that mixed-gender groups present.

Historically, women set out to create networks because they felt left out. Today women have perfected networking to such an extent in some communities that men actually ask to be admitted to exclusive women's groups. Women in Film faced and met that challenge by accepting men as members. Some of the industry men felt they were missing too much of the action.

Women Investing in Women

Networking has shown us that women do help women. In fact, most women will recount the numerous breaks they've had from other women.

WEALTHY WOMEN

In 1989, there were 1,427,500 women holding more than $600,000 in gross assets. These women privately held a total of $2.24 trillion.

Source: IRS 1989 survey data.

Recently, women networkers have realized potential female investors await. Women with money must be educated to make their own investment decisions. These decisions should include a healthy portion of women-led businesses. (No investor, unless highly experienced, should put more than 10 percent of her wealth at risk in start-up businesses or even later-stage businesses that are still considered "venture." The more conservative rule is 5 percent.)

Until we can grow more women entrepreneurs in recognized, publicly available venture locations, such as venture fairs, finding your best investment target—like-minded women—will require avid networking.

Is Networking Worth the Time It Takes?

"Women continue to find themselves disproportionately excluded from established business circles, where important knowledge is shared. Business networks, both formal and informal, share valuable information about business opportunities, problem solving, other contacts and business-generating activities."

—Center for Policy Alternatives

Networking enriches isolated lives in much the same way that quilting bees did on the frontier and the PTA did in the fifties.

Networking provides the social glue for women in disparate industries who because of their heavy schedules might never connect. Networking is inspiring. Networking is draining.

Most people who use networks, whether for capital or business contacts or information exchange, find the rewards worth the price.

In an important sense, networking has become for women a kind of formalized mentoring combined with a formalized effort to produce social change. In your case, that social change is closing the capital gap—by providing you with capital to implement your business plan.

Unless you have many friends with money to invest, we don't know of any other way to better help you both find and receive financing. Whether you choose to network exclusively with other women or specifically within your industry, one choice is clear—you need to network.

Resources and References

Everything you need to network for capital, from an informational standpoint, can be found at a large public library. From industry associations to locating like-minded businesses in your area, the leads are at the library.

If your formal education was completed before libraries were computerized, don't be intimidated by the new look of libraries today. Most the of the musty old files now dart across computers screens as databases. For example, if you want to research a topic in popular magazines, you'll find indexes of titles and article summaries on the computer. Many libraries allow you to print these short listings; therefore, you can save hours of hand-done research. By entering the correct search words, you can find just the information you need, from mother-daughter businesses to stuff like "Extra! Extra! Men and Women Are Different," the title of a recent article in *Inc.* magazine.

If you know a great deal about your industry, but you would like to locate other like-minded women, you have choices of industry organizations paralleling the generic ones, industry by industry; national women's groups; and state and local women's groups, either dedicated to a concept, such as the powerful National Association of Women's Business Owners (NAWBO), or to an area, such as the Women's Business Development Center in Chicago.

If you also belong to a minority, additional associations also address your needs. Some of these groups focus on race first, gender second. Others are women's groups for particular ethnic backgrounds, such as The Black Women's Network or MANA, A National Latina Organization.

The harder the industry is to break into, the greater the help industry associations may be. For example, in Hollywood, Women in

Film provides an avenue for women (and select men) to network in the entertainment industry, while the Hollywood Women's Political Committee combines Democratic fund-raising with high-powered networking. In Washington, the organization to join is The International Women's Forum. In New York, to break into high finance, locate the Financial Women's Association of New York.

Be sure to see *The Business Women's Network Directory: Profiles of the Top 400 U.S. Business and Professional Women's Organizations, 1995–1996* (Washington, DC: The Business Women's Network, 1996).

If you know your subject area—say, construction—then in addition to professional associations of construction entrepreneurs, such as the Federation of Women Contractors, you'd want to consider networking with other women, because within the industry women's numbers are scarce. You may find just the moral support you need to let off steam after a day of bossing (mostly) men around on the construction site.

Good manners will carry you a lot further in successful networking than any other single skill set. Former White House Social Secretary Letitia Baldridge's *New Complete Guide to Executive Manners* (New York: Rawson Associates, 1993) is the definitive book on executive manners. But of course, Emily Post's *Etiquette,* 12th Ed. (New York: Funk and Wagnalls, 1969) remains the classic in the field. For the Platonic ideal, read any pre-1970 edition of *Etiquette.*

Anne Baber's and Lynne Waymon's *52 Ways to Re-Connect, Follow Up & Stay in Touch...When You Don't Have Time to Network* (Dubuque, IA: Kendall/Hunt Publishing Company, 1994) and *Great Connections* (Dubuque, Iowa: Kendall/Hunt Publishing Company, 1991) are excellent books on the art of networking. Their new book, *Bottom-Line, Networking Know-How* is forthcoming in 1996.

Networking within ethnic bounds has also taken hold nationwide. *Minority Organizations: A National Directory* (Garrett Park, MD: Garrett Park Press, 1992). George Fraser's *Success Runs in Our Race* (New York: William Morrow, 1994) skillfully discusses effective networking in the African American community.

Government Statistics on
Women-Owned Businesses

The Results of the 1992 Business Census: Women Business Owners

NUMBER OF WOMEN-OWNED FIRMS

The number of women-owned firms has increased by 43 percent over the past five years, excluding C-corps. In 1992, when the survey was conducted, 6.4 million women-owned firms were counted. This represents almost double the rate of growth since 1987 of all firms during that period.

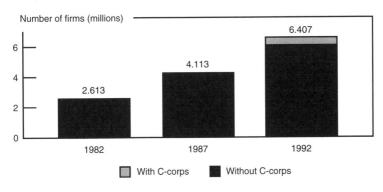

Source: U.S. Bureau of Census.

EMPLOYMENT BY WOMEN-OWNED FIRMS

Employment by women-owned firms has doubled in each of the last five years (inclusion of C-corporations doubles 1992 employment numbers). Between 1987 and 1992, employment by women-owned firms rose more than 100 percent, excluding C-corps, in a period in our history noted for recession, unemployment, and corporate streamlining and downsizing.

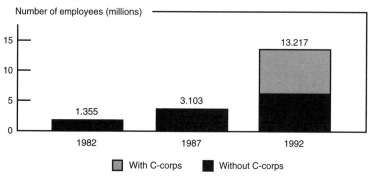

Source: U.S. Bureau of Census.

ANNUAL SALES OF WOMEN-OWNED FIRMS

Women-owned firms generated nearly $1.6 trillion in sales in 1992. Between 1987 and 1992, sales and receipts of women-owned companies increased by 131 percent to $1.6 trillion, exceeding all forecasts for this sector.

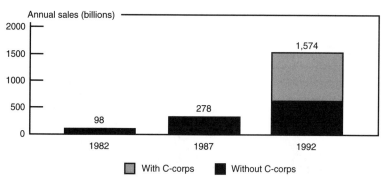

Source: U.S. Bureau of Census.

GROWTH IN WOMEN-OWNED FIRMS BY INDUSTRY*

The growth in the number of women-owned firms exceeds the national average in every state and in nearly every industry. The number of women-owned firms has grown in traditional and non-traditional industries alike. While women's firms still are predominantly in the service and retail sector, the greatest growth in the number of women-owned businesses has been in construction, wholesale trade, transportation, and manufacturing.

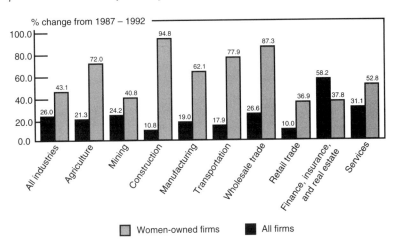

*Includes only sole proprietorships, partnerships, and subchapter S-corporations.

Source: U.S. Bureau of Census.

WOMEN-OWNED BUSINESS DOLLARS BY STATE ($000)

	Fiscal Year 1994	*Fiscal Year 1993*
Alabama	$69,451	$74,699
Alaska	14,749	13,112
Arizona	47,705	29,368
Arkansas	9,371	6,094
California	163,835	153,483
Colorado	52,882	48,827
Connecticut	954	2,160
Delaware	788	988
District of Columbia	471,063	389,715

(continues)

WOMEN-OWNED BUSINESS DOLLARS BY STATE ($000) (*cont'd*)

	Fiscal Year 1994	Fiscal Year 1993
Florida	68,545	54,394
Georgia	75,927	68,213
Hawaii	19,689	17,712
Idaho	11,353	7,701
Illinois	62,175	70,992
Indiana	3,657	3,609
Iowa	1,696	298
Kansas	7,935	5,905
Kentucky	19,963	15,806
Louisiana	16,458	11,751
Maine	33	306
Maryland	80,329	128,978
Massachusetts	14,769	14,763
Michigan	8,254	22,353
Minnesota	2,943	2,007
Mississippi	27,007	16,775
Missouri	57,056	46,402
Montana	6,361	8,926
Nebraska	6,739	19,996
Nevada	8,010	12,249
New Hampshire	333	467
New Jersey	34,671	45,830
New Mexico	23,247	20,039
New York	63,472	54,718
North Carolina	28,331	15,378
North Dakota	2,333	2,981
Ohio	103,096	103,942
Oklahoma	46,942	42,334
Oregon	15,073	6,483
Pennsylvania	121,571	84,570
Rhode Island	4,029	5,223
South Carolina	61,165	42,479
South Dakota	3,386	9,466
Tennessee	36,128	34,401
Texas	116,262	94,219
Utah	7,444	6,294
Vermont	319	833
Virginia	288,760	182,658
West Virginia	6,373	4,654
Washington	48,423	75,706
Wisconsin	6,579	4,370
Wyoming	515	271

PERCENT GROWTH OF WOMEN-OWNED BUSINESSES BY STATE, 1987–1992

In each of the 50 states, the growth in women-owned businesses exceeded the growth of all businesses. In nine states, the percentage growth of women-owned firms was double that of all firms in each of those states.

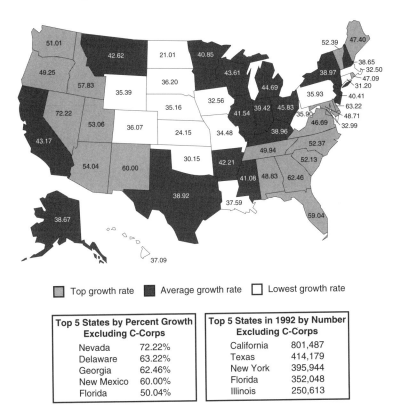

■ Top growth rate   ■ Average growth rate   □ Lowest growth rate

Top 5 States by Percent Growth Excluding C-Corps	
Nevada	72.22%
Delaware	63.22%
Georgia	62.46%
New Mexico	60.00%
Florida	50.04%

Top 5 States in 1992 by Number Excluding C-Corps	
California	801,487
Texas	414,179
New York	395,944
Florida	352,048
Illinois	250,613

WOMEN-OWNED SMALL BUSINESS SHARE OF FEDERAL CONTRACTS* (BILLIONS OF DOLLARS)

	Fiscal Year 1992	Fiscal Year 1993	Fiscal Year 1994
Prime Contract Dollars	$2,908	$3,239	$3,467
Subcontract Dollars	$1,069	$1,363	$1,453
Total Dollar Awards	$3,977	$4,602	$4,920

*The Federal Contract Awards to Women-Owned Small Businesses increased by $625 million from fiscal year 1992 to fiscal year 1993 and increased by $318 million from fiscal year 1992 to fiscal year 1994. The total increase from fiscal year 1992 to fiscal year 1994 was nearly $1 billion.

SMALL BUSINESS SHARE OF FEDERAL CONTRACTS (BILLIONS OF DOLLARS)

	Fiscal Year 1992	Fiscal Year 1993	Fiscal Year 1994
Prime Contract Dollars	$41,331	$42,237	$42,302
Subcontract Dollars	$22,324	$20,782	$22,003
Total Dollar Awards	$63,655	$63,019	$62,305
Percentage WOB Awards	6.2%	7.3%	7.7%

Source: U.S. Small Business Administration, Office of Government Contracting, unpublished data, 1992–1994.

FEDERAL CONTRACT ACTIONS OVER $25,000
By Industry, Fiscal Year 1994

Women-Owned Business Dollars (Total Dollars: $2,508,052)

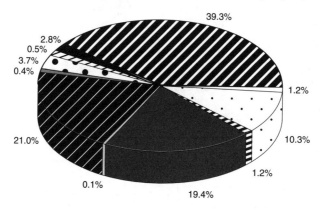

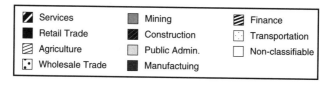

Services | Mining | Finance
Retail Trade | Construction | Transportation
Agriculture | Public Admin. | Non-classifiable
Wholesale Trade | Manufactuing |

Small Business Dollars (Total Dollars: 28,520,213)

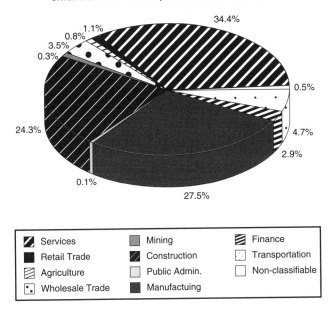

Services

Retail Trade

Agriculture

Wholesale Trade

Mining

Construction

Public Admin.

Manufactuing

Finance

Transportation

Non-classifiable

Source: Federal Procurement Data Center, June 1995; prepared by SBA Office of Government Contracting, unpublished data.

APPENDIX 2

Government Contact

Locations

National Women's Business Council Member List

Lillian Vernon, Chair, NWBC
Founder and President
Lillian Vernon Corporation
New Rochelle, New York

Raydean Acevedo, President & CEO
Research Management Consultants
McLean, Virginia

Muriel Siebert, President
Muriel Siebert & Company
Manhattan, New York

Ella Williams, President and CEO
Aegir Systems
Oxnard, California

Cheryl Womack, President & CEO
VCW, Inc.
Kansas City, Missouri

Association for Enterprise
Opportunity
Kathy Keeley, Chair
Minneapolis, Minnesota

National Association for Female
Executives
Wendy Reid Crisp, Executive Director
New York, New York

National Association of Women
Business Owners
Margaret Smith, President-Elect
Silver Spring, Maryland

National Council of Negro Women,
Inc.
Grenda Girton, Assoc. Executive
Director
Washington, D.C.

Women's Business Development
Center
Hedy Ratner, Director
Chicago, Illinois

Executive Director
Amy Millman

Deputy Director
Juliette Tracey

Inter-Agency Committee on Women's Business Enterprise

Chair:	Laura D'Andrea Tyson Assistant to the President for Economic Policy National Economic Council
	Elizabeth Myers, Deputy Assistant to the President Director for Women's Initiatives and Outreach The White House
Commerce:	Gloria Gutierrez, Deputy Assistant Secretary U.S. Department of the Air Force
Executive Office of the President:	Alexis Herman, Assistant to the President Office of Public Liaison The White House
Federal Reserve:	Janet Yellen, Governor
General Services Administration:	Barbara Silby, Chief of Staff Office of the Administrator
Health and Human Services:	Secretary Donna Shalala Sarah Kovner, Special Assistant to the Secretary
Labor:	Karen Nussbaum, Director Women's Bureau
Small Business Administration:	Ellen Thrasher, Acting Assistant Administrator Office of Women's Business Ownership
Transportation:	Jolene Molitoris, Administrator Federal Railroad Administration
Treasury:	Darcy Bradbury, Deputy Assistant Secretary Office for Domestic Finance

U.S. Small Business Administration's Business Information Centers (BICs) 1995

U.S. Small Business Administration
Atlanta District Office
1720 Peachtree Road NW, 6th floor
Atlanta, GA 30309
(404) 347-4749
(404) 347-2355 fax

U.S. Small Business Administration
Business Information Center
3600 Wilshire Boulevard, Suite L100
Los Angeles, CA 90010
(213) 251-7253
(213) 251-7255 fax

Business Information Center
121 S. Meramec Avenue
Lobby Level
St. Louis, MO 63105
(314) 854-6861
(314) 889-7687 fax

U.S. Small Business Administration
Seattle District Office
1200 Sixth Avenue, Suite 1700
Seattle, WA 98101-1128
(206) 553-7310
(206) 553-7099 fax

U.S. Small Business Administration
Houston District Office
9301 Southwest Freeway, Suite 550
Houston, Texas 77074-1591
(713) 773-6545
(713) 773-6550 fax

SBA/NationsBank/MBDA
Small Business Resource Center
3401 West End Avenue
Nashville, TN 37203
(615) 749-4000
(615) 749-3685 fax

U.S. Small Business Administration
Chicago District Office
500 W. Madison Street, Suite 1250
Chicago, Il 60661-2511
(312) 353-1825
(312) 886-5688 fax

U.S. Small Business Administration
Boston District Office
10 Causeway Street, Room 265
Boston, MA 02222-1093
(617) 565-5615
(617) 565-5598 fax

U.S. Small Business Administration
Kansas District Office
323 West 8th Street, Suite 104
Kansas City, MO 64105
(816) 374-6675
(816) 374-6759 fax

SBA/Bell Atlantic
Business Information Center
Washington District Office
1110 Vermont Avenue NW, Suite 900
Washington, DC 20043-4500
(202) 606-4000 ext. 266
(202) 606-4225 fax

Women's Procurement Pilot Program

WOMEN'S ADVOCATES

U.S. Department of Agriculture
Ms. Sharon Harris
Office of Small and Disadvantaged
Business Utilization
Washington, D.C. 20250
(202) 720-7117

U.S. Department of Defense
Ms. Dora H. Thomas
OUSD (A&T) SADBU 361 Defense
Pentagon
Washington, D.C. 20301-3061
(703) 697-9383

U.S. Department of Energy
Ms. Gloria Smith
Office of Impact
1000 Independence Avenue SW
Washington, D.C. 20585
(202) 586-8383

U.S. Department of Health & Human
Services
Ms. Y. Angel Graves
Office of Small & Disadvantaged
Business Utilization
Washington, D.C. 20201
(202) 690-6670

U.S. Department of Housing & Urban Development
Mr. Joseph Piljay
Washington, D.C. 20585
(202) 708-1428

U.S. Department of Justice
Mr. Joseph K. Bryan
Office of Small & Disadvantaged Business Utilization
ARB Room 3235
Washington, D.C. 20530
(202) 616-0521

U.S. Department of Labor
Ms. June Robinson
Office of Small Business & Minority Affairs
200 Constitution Avenue NW, Room C2318
Washington, D.C. 20210
(202) 219-9148

U.S. Department of Transportation
Ms. Luz Hopewell
Office of Small & Disadvantaged Business Utilization
Washington, D.C. 20590
(202) 366-1930

Environmental Protection Agency
Ms. Margie Wilson
Office of Small & Disadvantaged Business Utilization
Washington, D.C. 20460
(703) 305-7305

General Services Administration
Ms. Elizabeth Ivey
18th and F Streets
Washington, D.C. 20405
(202) 501-4466

National Aeronautics & Space Administration
Ms. Rae C. Marter
Headquarters
Washington, D.C. 20546-0001
(202) 358-2088

Women's Business

Associations

National Coalition of Women's Business Organizations

Alliance for Women Business Owners
Charlotte Taylor, Executive Director
900 Second Street NE, Suite 205
Washington, DC 20002
(202) 543-1200
(202) 543-7534 fax

American Association of University Women
Anne Bryant, Executive Director
Nancy Zurkin [(202) 785-7720]
1111 16th Street NW, 3rd floor
Washington, DC 20036
(202) 785-7788
(202) 872-1425 fax

American Business Women's Association
Carolyn Elman, Executive Director
P.O. Box 8728
Kansas City, MO 64114-0728
(816) 361-6621
(816) 361-4991 fax

American Women's Economic Development Corporation (AWED)**
Suzanne Tufts, President and Executive Director
71 Vanderbilt Avenue, Suite 320
New York, NY 10169
(212) 692-9100
(212) 692-9296 fax

AWED - Connecticut**
Bi-County Community Action Programs, Inc.
Fran Polak, Director of Training and Counseling
Plaza West Office Centers
2001 W. Main Street, Suite 140
Stamford, CT 06902
(203) 326-7914
(203) 326-7916 fax

*National Women's Business Council Members
**SBA Office of Women's Business Ownership Demonstration Sites

AWED - Irvine, California**
Linda Harasin
Acting Executive Director
2301 Campus Drive, Suite 20
Irvine, CA 92715
(714) 474-2933
(714) 474-7416 fax

AWED - Long Beach, California**
Phil Borden
Regional Director
100 West Broadway, Suite 500
Long Beach, CA 90802
(310) 983-3747
(310) 983-3750 fax

AWED - Washington, DC
Claire Wojno
1250 24th Street NW, Suite 120
Washington, DC 20037
(202) 857-0091
(202) 223-2775 fax

An Income of Her Own
Joline Godfrey
406 Lion Street
Ojai, CA 93023
(805) 646-1215
(805) 646-4206 fax

Ann Arbor Community Development
Corporation**
Michelle Vazquez
2008 Hogback Road, Suite 2A
Ann Arbor, MI 48105
(313) 677-1400
(313) 677-1465 fax

Asian American Professional
Women Inc.**
Mei Chan, Bonnie Wong
125 Lafayette Street
New York, NY 10013
(212) 966-7888
(212) 966-8988 fax

Association of Black Women
Entrepreneurs, Inc.
Dolores Ratcliffe, Chair
P.O. Box 49368
Los Angeles, CA 90049
(213) 624-8639

Association for Enterprise
Opportunity*
Kathy Keeley, Chair
Chris Benuzzi, Executive Director
70 E. Lake Street, Suite 520
Chicago, IL 60601-5907
(312) 357-0177
(312) 357-0180 fax

The Briles Group
Judith Briles
P.O. Box 22021
Denver, CO 80222-0021
(303) 745-4590
(303) 745-4595 fax

Business Women's Network
Kent Christian, Project Director
Nicole Johnson, Project Director
1146 19th Street NW, 3rd floor
Washington, DC 20036
(202) 466-8209
(202) 833-1808 fax

Capital Missions Company -
Capital Circle
Susan Davis, President
31W007 North Avenue, Suite 101
West Chicago, IL 60185
(708) 876-1101
(708) 876-0187 fax

Catalyst
Sheila Wellington, President
250 Park Avenue South
New York, NY 10003
(212) 777-8900
(212) 477-4252 fax

Center for Policy Alternatives
Linda Tarr-Whelan, President and
Executive Director
Rich Ferlauto, Associate Director
Jamie Cooper, Associate Director
1875 Connecticut Avenue NW,
Suite 710
Washington, DC 20009
(202) 387-6030
(202) 986-2539 fax

Center for Women's Business
Enterprise (CWBE)**
Susan Spencer, Austin Site
Coordinator
508 Ladin Lane
Augsin, TX 78734
(512) 261-8525
(512) 261-8525 fax

CWBE - Houston**
Linda Schneider, Coordinator
2425 West Loop South, Suite 1004
Houston, TX 77027
(713) 552-1267
(713) 578-8485 fax

Center for Women and
Enterprise, Inc.
Andrea Silbert, Susan Hammond
45 Bromfield Street
Boston, MA 02108
(617) 423-3001

Chamber Women's Business
Initiative**
Linda Steward, Director
37 North High Street
Columbus, OH 43215
(614) 225-6082
(614) 469-8250 fax

Coalition of 100 Black Women**
Leah Creque-Harris, Project Director
The Candler Building
127 Peachtree Street NE, Suite 700
Atlanta, GA 30303
(404) 659-4008
(404) 659-3001 fax

Coastal Enterprises, Inc.**
Ellen Golden
P.O. Box 268
Wiscasset, ME 04578
(207) 882-7552
(207) 882-7308 fax

Colorado Women's Economic
Development Council
Elaine Demery, Chair
2121 S. Oneida Street, Suite 150
Denver, CO 80224
(303) 753-6100

Committee of 200
Michele Hooper, President
Lydia Lewis, Executive Director
625 N. Michigan Avenue, Suite 500
Chicago, IL 60611
(312) 751-3477
(312) 943-9401 fax

*National Women's Business Council Members
**SBA Office of Women's Business Ownership Demonstration Sites

Dialogue on Diversity
Christina Caballero, President
1730 K Street NW, Suite 304
Washington, DC 20006
(703) 631-0650
(703) 631-0617 fax

Dingman Center for
Entrepreneurship
Dr. Charles O. Heller
College of Business and Management
University of Maryland
College Park, MD 20742-1815
(301) 405-2144
(301) 314-9152 fax

EMPOWER Pyramid Career Services**
Andrea Zalantis, Director
2400 Cleveland Avenue NW
Canton, OH 44709
(216) 453-3767
(216) 453-6079 fax

Enterprise Center/Women's
Business Center**
Betty Reese, Coordinator
129 E. Main Street
Hillsboro, OH 45133
(513) 393-9599
(513) 393-8159 fax

The Entrepreneur's Network for
Women**
Becky Doarr, Business Specialist
Kay Tachakert, Information Systems
100 South Maple
P.O. Box 81
Watertown, SD 57201
(605) 882-5080 or (800) 499-7404
(605) 882-5069 fax

EXCEL!**
Carol Lopucki, Executive Director
Eberhard Center
301 W. Fulton, Room 718
Grand Rapids, MI 49504
(616) 771-6693

Federation of Women Contractors
Judy DeAngelo, President
Carol Bulawa, Secretary
Kathleen Calls, Executive Director
117 N. Jefferson, Suite 201
Chicago, IL 60661
(312) 665-0033

Financial Women International
Martha Tabio, Int'l. President
Gale Wood, Executive Director
200 N. Glebe Road, Suite 814
Arlington, VA 22203
(703) 807-2007
(703) 807-0111 fax

Financial Women's Association of NY
Gail Miner, President
Nancy Sellar, Executive Director
215 Park Avenue South, Suite 2010
New York, NY 10003
(212) 533-2141
(212) 982-3008 fax

FINCA International
Donna Fabiani
1101 14th Street NW, 11th floor
Washington, DC 20005
(202) 682-1510
(202) 682-1535 fax

Forum for Intercultural
Communication
Maureitte Hurah-Cesar,
Executive Director
2400 Virginia Avenue NW
Washington, DC 20037-2601
(202) 775-7234
(202) 223-1699 fax

Institute for Women's Policy Research
Heidi Hartmann, President
1400 20th Street NW, Suite 104
Washington, DC 20036
(202) 785-5100
(202) 833-4362 fax

The International Alliance, Inc.
Evln Willman, President
c/o Willman & Company
1809 Art Museum Drive, Suite 10
Jacksonville, FL 32207
(904) 396-9344
(904) 396-9348 fax

International Network of Women
in Technology
Carolyn Leighton, Executive Director
4641 Burnet Avenue
Sherman Oaks, CA 91403
(818) 990-1987

International Women's Forum
Susan Greenwood, President
Lilly Richardella
1146 19th Street NW, Suite 600
Washington, DC 20036
(202) 775-8917
(202) 429-0271 fax

Kauffman Foundation
Center for Entrepreneurial
Leadership, Inc.
Trish Costello, Director Kauffman
Fellows Program
4900 Oak Street
Kansas City, MO 64112-2776
(816) 932-1000
(816) 932-1100 fax

LAMA
Marina Morales Laverdy
419 New Jersey Avenue, SE
Washington, DC 20003
(202) 546-3803
(202) 546-3807 fax

MANA - A National Latina Organization
Elisa Sanchez, President
Laura Campos, Executive Director
1725 K Street NW, Suite 501
Washington, DC 20006
(202) 833-0060
(202) 496-0588 fax

Mi Casa, Business Center for
Women**
Luz Cofresi-Howe, Director
Wendy Krajewaki-Kenar
571 Galapago Street
Denver, CO 80204
(303) 573-1302
(303) 595-0422 fax

Montana Women's Capital Fund**
Kelly Flaherty
54 North Last Chance Gulch
Helena, MT 59624
(406) 443-3144
(406) 442-1789 fax

Ms. Foundation for Women
Marie Wilson, President
Sara Gould, Director of the Economic
Development Program
120 Wall Street, 33rd floor
New York, NY 10005
(212) 742-2300
(212) 742-1653 fax

National Association of Black Women
Entrepreneurs
Marilyn French Hubbard,
Founder/President
P.O. Box 1375
Detroit, MI 48231
(810) 356-3686
(810) 354-3793 fax

*National Women's Business Council Members
**SBA Office of Women's Business Ownership Demonstration Sites

National Association of Female
Executives*
Rebecca Darwin, COO
Leslie Smith, Executive Director
30 Irving Place, 5th Floor
New York, NY 10003
(212) 477-2200
(212) 477-8215 fax

National Association of Negro
Business & Professional Women's
Clubs, Inc.
Julianne Malveaux, President
Sheila Quarles, Executive Director
1806 New Hampshire Avenue NW
Washington, DC 20009
(202) 483-4206
(202) 462-7253 fax

National Association of Women
Business Advocates
Mollie Cole, President
c/o Department of Commerce/
Community Affairs
100 West Randolph, Suite 3400
Chicago, IL 60601
(312) 814-7176
(312) 814-2807 fax

National Association of Women
Business Owners (NAWBO)*
Margaret Smith, President
Caren Wilcox, Executive Director
1100 Wayne Avenue, Suite 830
Silver Spring, MD 20910
(301) 608-2590
(301) 608-2596 fax

NAWBO/EXCEL! Women Mean
Business
Mary Burt, Executive Director
600 West Lafayette
Detroit, MI 48226
(313) 961-4748
(313) 961-5434 fax

NAWBO of New Jersey - EXCEL**
Harriet Nazarete, Project Director
225 Hamilton Street
Bound Brook, NJ 08805-2042
(908) 560-9607
(908) 560-9687 fax

NAWBO Pittsburgh**
Carmelle Nickens, Director
657 California Avenue
Pittsburgh, PA 15201
(412) 521-4735
(412) 521-4737 fax

NAWBO of St. Louis**
Irina Bronstein, Project Director
222 S. Berniston, Suite 216
St. Louis, MO 63105
(314) 863-0046
(314) 863-2079 fax

National Association of Women in
Construction (NAWIC)
Susan Levy CCA, President
Executive Director
327 South Adams Street
Fort Worth, TX 76104
(817) 877-5551
(817) 877-0324 fax

National Association of Women's
Yellow Pages
Michelle Schaefer, President
7358 N. Lincoln, Suite 150
Chicago, IL 60646
(708) 679-7800
(708) 679-7845 fax

National Center for American Indian
Enterprise Development**
Vera Pooyouma, Marilyn Andrews,
Steven L.A. Stallings
553 E. Juanita Street
Mesa, AZ 85204
(602) 545-1298
(602) 545-4208 fax
serving Arizona, Washington and
California

National Chambers of Commerce for
Women
Maggie Rinaldi, Chair
10 Waterside Plaza, Suite 6-H
New York, NY 10010
(212) 685-3454
NO FAX

National Coalition of 100 Black
Women, Inc.
Jewell Jackson McCabe, Chair
Shirley Poole, Executive Director
38 W. 32nd Street, Suite 1610
New York, NY 10001
(212) 947-2196
(212) 947-2477 fax

National Congress of Neighborhood
Women
Ronnie Feit, Board Member
604 7th Street SW
Washington, DC 20024
(202) 484-2187
(202) 863-2943 fax

National Council of Negro Women,
Inc.*, **
Dorothy Height, President and CEO
Brenda Girton, Associate Executive
Director
Eleanor Hinton-Hoytt, Project Director
633 Pennsylvania SW
Washington, DC 20004
(202) 463-6680
(202) 628-0233 fax

National Education Center for
Women in Business
Barbara Mystick, Director
Seton Hill Drive
Greensburg, PA 15601
(412) 830-4625
(412) 834-7131 fax

National Federation of Black Women
Business Owners
Mary Walker, President
1500 Massachusetts Avenue NW,
Suite 5
Washington, DC 20005
(202) 833-3450
(202) 331-7822 fax

National Federation of Business and
Professional Women's Blucs, Inc.
Audrey Jaynes, Executive Director
2012 Massachusetts Avenue NW
Washington, DC 20036
(202) 293-1100
(202) 861-0298 fax

National Foundation for Women
Business Owners
Susan Peterson, Chair
Sharon Hadary, Executive Director
1100 Wayne Avenue, Suite 830
Silver Spring, MD 20910
(301) 495-4975
(301) 495-4979 fax

National Foundation for Women
Legislators
Bonnie Sue Cooper, President
Robin Read, Executive Director
3240 Prospect Street NW
Washington, DC 20007
(202) 337-3565
(202) 337-3566 fax

National Network of Commercial Real
Estate Women (CREW)
Anne De Voe Lawler, President
Linda Holleman, Executive Director
3115 W. 6th Street, Suite C-122
Lawrence, KS 66049
(913) 832-1808
(913) 832-1551 fax

*National Women's Business Council Members
**SBA Office of Women's Business Ownership Demonstration Sites

National Women's Economic Alliance
Foundation
Patricia De Stacey Harrison
1440 New York Avenue NW,
Suite 300
Washington, DC 20005
(202) 393-5257
(202) 639-8685 fax

Nevada Self-Employment Trust**
Janice Barbour, Director
560 Mill Street
Reno, NV 89502
(702) 329-6789
(702) 329-6738 fax

New Mexico Woman's Purchasing
Council
Jan Zimmerman
P.O. Box 6706
Albuquerque, NM 87197-6706
(505) 344-4230
(505) 345-4128 fax

North Texas Women's Business Development Center, Inc.**
Bill J. Priest Institute for Economic
Development
Heather Day Ballinger
1402 Corinth Street
Dallas, TX 75215-2111
(214) 428-1177
(214) 855-4300 fax

Northwest Ohio Women's
Entrepreneurial Network**
Linda Fayerweather
Director, Toledo Area Chamber of
Commerce
300 Madison Avenue, Suite 200
Toledo, OH 43604
(419) 243-8191
(419) 241-8302 fax

Ohio Women's Business Resource
Network**
Mary Ann McClure, Coordinator
77 South High Street, 28th Floor
Columbus, OH 43266
(614) 466-2682
(614) 466-0829 fax

Soroptimist International
of the Americas
Patsy Daniels, President
2 Penn Center Plaza, Suite 1000
Philadelphia, PA 19012

Southeast Louisiana Black Chamber
of Commerce**
(works with WEED)
Valentine Pierce
1600 Canal Street, Suite 606
New Orleans, LA 70112
(504) 539-9450
(504) 539-9499 fax

Southern Oregon Women's Access to
Credit**
Mary O'Kief
33 North Central, Suite 410
Medford, OR 97510
(503) 779-3992
(503) 779-3992 fax

Utah Technology Finance
Corporation**
Susan Bastian
177 East 100 South
Salt Lake City, UT 84111
(801) 364-4346
(801) 364-4361 fax

Washington Transportation Seminar
Peggy Briggs
Perry-Briggs Business Services
3200 Brooklawn Terrace
Chevy Chase, MD 20815
(301) 657-3492
(301) 657-3492 fax

WBE Line
Regina McManus, President
4253 Montgomery Road
Ellicott City, MD 21043
(410) 465-6399
(410) 750-8834 fax

WESST Company**
Women's Economic Self-Sufficiency
Team
Agnes Noonan, Executive Director
414 Silver Southwest
Albuquerque, NM 87102
(505) 848-4760
(505) 241-4766 fax

WESST Corporation** - Taos, NM
Yolanda Nunez, Project Director
Taos County Economic Development
P.O. Box 1389
Taos, NM 87571
(505) 758-3099
(505) 758-8153 fax

WEST Company** (A Women's
Economic Self-Sufficiency Training
Program)
Carol Steele
340 North Main Street
Fort Bragg, CA 95437
(707) 964-7571
(707) 961-1340 fax

WEST Company ** (not funded)
Sheilah Rogers, Director
367 North State Street, Suite 206
Ukish, CA 95482
(707) 468-3553
(707) 462-8945 fax

Wisconsin Women
Entrepreneurs, Inc.
Victoria Finelli-Jasiek, President
6949 N. 100th Street
Milwaukee, WI
(414) 358-9290

Wisconsin Women
Entrepreneurs, Inc.**
Karen Hendrickson, Member
Services Co.
6949 North 100th Street
Milwaukee, WI 53224
(414) 358-9290
(414) 358-9261 fax

Wisconsin Women's Business
Initiative Corporation**
Wendy Werkmeister
1915 North Dr. Martin Luther King
Jr. Drive
Milwaukee, WI 53212
(414) 372-2070
(414) 372-2083 fax

Women Business Owners
Corporation**
Kathleen Schwallie
18 Encanto Drive
Rolling Hills Estates, CA 90274
(310) 530-0582
(310) 530-1483 fax

Women Construction Owners &
Executives, USA
Rosemary Briner, President
Shirley Blase, Executive Director
1615 New Hampshire Avenue NW,
Suite 402
Washington, DC 20009
(202) 745-9263

*National Women's Business Council Members
**SBA Office of Women's Business Ownership Demonstration Sites

Women Entrepreneurs, Inc.**
(not funded)
Peg Moertl, Executive Director
Bartlett Building
36 East 4th Street, Suite 925
Cincinnati, OH 45202

mailing address:
P.O. Box 2662
Cincinnati, OH 45201-2662
(513) 684-0700
(513) 665-2452 fax

Women First National Legislative
Committee
622 North Tazewell Street
Arlington, VA 22203
(703) 522-6121
(703) 276-3583 fax

Women in Cable &
Telecommunications, Inc.
Ann Carlsen, President
Pamela Williams, Executive Director
230 West Monroe
Chicago, IL 60606
(312) 634-2330
(312) 634-2345 fax

Women in New Development
Ann McGill
BI-CAP, Inc
P.O. Box 579
Bemidji, MN 56601
(218) 751-4631
(218) 751-8452 fax

Women Incorporated
Lindsey Johnson
Judith Luther Wilder
1401 21st Street, Suite 310
Sacramento, CA 95814
(916) 448-8444
(916) 448-8898 fax

Women's Business Center
White Earth Reservation Tribal
Council
Mary Turner, Director
202 South Main Street
P.O. Box 478
Mahnomen, MN 56557
(218) 935-2827 / (800) 793-7535
218-935-2390 fax

Women's Business Council
Shreveport Chamber of Commerce
Martha Marak, President
P.O. Box 20074
Shreveport, LA 71120-0074
(318) 677-2553
(318) 677-2534 fax

Women's Business Development
Center*, **
Christine Kurtz-White, Director
Florida International University,
OET-3
University Park
Miami, Fl 33199
(305) 348-3951
(305) 348-2931 fax

Women's Business Development
Center*,**
Hedy Ratner, Director
Linda Darragh
8 South Michigan Avenue, Suite 400
Chicago, IL 60603
(312) 853-3477
(312) 853-0145 fax

Women's Business Development Center^^
Geri Swift
1315 Walnut Street, Suite 1116
Philadelphia, PA 19107
(215) 790-9232
(215) 790-9231 fax

Women's Business Institute**
Penny P. Retzer, Director
901 Page Drive
P.O. Box 9238
Fargo, ND 58106
(701) 235-6488
(701) 235-8284 fax

Women's Business Resource Program of S.E. Ohio**
Debra McBride, Project Director
Technology & Enterprise Building
20 East Circle Drive, Suite 190
Athens, OH 45701
(614) 593-1797
(614) 564-2801 fax

Women's Collateral Funding Inc.
Nina Brown, President
1529 Walnut Street, 4th Floor
Philadelphia, PA 19102
(215) 564-2800
(215) 564-2801 fax

Women's Credit and Finance Project
Dr. Emily Card, Director
P.O. Box 3725
Santa Monica, CA 90403
(310) 315-2880
(310) 315-5422 fax

Women's Development Center**
Tracie Haynes, Director
300 N. Abbe Road
Elyria, OH 44035
(216) 366-0770
(216) 366-0769 fax

Women's Initiative for Self Employment (WISE)**
(not funded)
Paulette Meyer, Interim Executive Director
450 Mission Street, Suite 402
San Francisco, CA 94105
(415) 247-9473
(415) 247-9471 fax

WISE** - Oakland, California
Helen Branham, Project Director
519 17th Street, Suite 520
Oakland, CA 94612
(510) 208-9473
(510) 208-9471 fax

Women's Legal Defense Fund
Judith Lichtman, President
1875 Connecticut Avenue NW, Suite 710
Washington, DC 20009
(202) 986-2600
(202) 986-2539 fax

Women's Network, Inc**
Marlene Miller, Director of Mentoring Programs
1540 West Market Street, Suite 100
Akron, OH 44313
(216) 864-5636
(216) 864-6526 fax

*National Women's Business Council Members
**SBA Office of Women's Business Ownership Demonstration Sites

Women's Opportunity and Resource
Development, Inc.**
Kelly Rosenleaf, Director
Rosalie Cates, Project Director
127 North Higgins
Missoula, MT 59802
(406) 543-3550
(406) 721-4584 fax

Women's Self-Employment Project
Connie Evans, President
20 North Clark Street, Suite 400
Chicago, IL 60602
(312) 606-8255
(312) 606-9215 fax

Women's World Banking
Nancy Barry, President
8 West 40th Street
New York, NY 10018
(212) 768-8513
(212) 768-8519 fax

Working Women's Money
University**
Lori Smith
3501 NW 63rd, Suite 609
Oklahoma City, OK 73116
(405) 842-1196
(405) 842-5067 fax

Zonta International
Barbara Geil, Acting Executive
Director
557 West Randolph Street
Chicago, IL 60661
(312) 930-5848
(312) 930-0951 fax

Venture Capital Resources

VENTURE FAIRS

Fair	Location	Length	# Presenters	Cost	Telephone
Arizona Venture Capital Conference	Phoenix, AZ	8 hrs.	NA	$225, $175 early	(602) 495-6461
Venture Capital Forum	Cambridge, MA	8 hrs.	NA	$25 reg. $75 non	NA
Florida Venture Capital Conference	Miami, FL	24 hrs.	19	$299, $249 early	(305) 446-5060
Utah Venture Capital Conference	Salt Lake, UT	8 hrs.	NA	$250	(801) 595-1141
Venture Capital in the Rockies	Denver, CO	24 hrs.	15–20	$395	(303) 296-2323
Los Angeles Technology Venture Forum	Los Angeles, CA	8 hrs.	15	$350, $250 early	(213) 622-7100
South Jersey Venture Fair	Cherry Hill, NJ	8 hrs.	40	$95 ($150 pres)	(609) 365-1300
North Coast Capital and Tech. Showcase	Cleveland, OH	24 hrs	30	$325 early	NA
Delaware Valley Venture Group	Philadelphia, PA	lunch	NA	$35, $55, $60	(215) 972-3989
Innovative Concepts Tech. and Business	Denver, CO	24 hrs.		25-35	NA
Texas Investment Forum	Austin, TX	24 hrs.	25		(713) 237-5700
Long Island Capital Forum,	Melville, NY	8 hrs.	20	$60, $75 ($200 pres)	(516) 423-9377
Investor Conference MA Telecomm. Council	Boston, MA	8 hrs.	35	$225	NA
Pittsburgh Growth Capital Conference	Pittsburgh, PA	24 hrs.	30	$275–$350	(412) 578-3481
Connecticut Venture Fair	Stamford, CT	8 hrs.	25	$245, $195	(203) 333-3CVG
Greater Washington Venture Fair	D.C. Metro	8 hrs.	25	$300, $200	(703) 903-5000

Source: Silbey & Co.

Other Resources for
Entrepreneurs

BUSINESS, INVESTMENT, AND FINANCE MAGAZINES

Barron's National Business & Financial Weekly
Best's Insurance Management Reports
Black Enterprise
Business America
Business Week

Changing Times
Commerce Business Daily
Communication Arts

Economic and Business Outlook
Economic Indicators
Economist
Entrepreneur

Federal Reserve Bulletin
Financial World
Forbes
Fortune
Futures
Futurist

Harvard Business Review
Hispanic Business

IMF Survey
Inc.
Industry Week
Investors Business Daily

Journal of Accountancy
Journal of Commerce

Journal of Economic Perspectives
Journal of Small Business Management

Kiplinger's Personal Finance
Kiplinger's Washington Newsletter

Money
Monthly Labor Review
Moody's (various publications)

Nation's Business

Occupational Outlook Quarterly
Outlook (Standard & Poor's)

Personnel Journal
Public Management
Public Relations Journal

Red Herring

Sales & Marketing Management
Savings and Community Banker
Standard & Poor's (various publications)

Success
Survey of Current Business

Trendline Daily Action

Value Line Investment Survey

APPENDIX 6

Contacting the Authors

The authors invite your correspondence. We can be reached at:

Emily Card and Adam Miller
P.O. Box 3725
Santa Monica, CA 90403
Tel: (310) 315-2880
Fax: (310) 315-5422

or you can visit our home page on the Internet at:

   http://www.womenmoney.com

or e-mail us at bizcapital@womenmoney.com or bizcapital@aol.com